Surviving Technology

Lessons from Theater: The New Necessities

For Living a Human Life

Paul Woodruff

Tibidabo Publishing
New York

To my six grandchildren,

this book is dedicated,

for their love of theater and of life.

Published by Tibidabo Publishing, Inc. New York

Cover art by Raimon Guirado

First published: January 2024

Visit our Quick Immersions Series on our Web:
www.quickimmersions.com

ISBN: 978-1-949845-37-2
1 2 3 4 5 6 7 8 9 10
Library of Congress Control Number: 2023952241
Printed in the United States of America.

Surviving Technology

Lessons from Theater: The New Necessities

For Living a Human Life

Paul Woodruff

Tibidabo Publishing
New York

Prologue

I am performing a chorale by Bach for an audience, at their request. They are filling up the small cabin, so I am on the porch. Trees rustle around me, and the lake ripples nearby. My instrument is a recorder, a wooden flute-like instrument that Bach knew well. The chorale I am performing is sacred to me, "O Jesu so sweet." I play it slowly and with all the reverent expression I can call from my instrument. I am launching into the second line of the piece when I hear a laugh from the cabin.

This is terribly wrong. Why are they laughing? I have not missed a note of this sacred music. Is reverence a joke? Perhaps they are not laughing at me but at a remark one of them has made about something else. Either way, they are not paying attention to my performance. I cannot see them in the cabin because the sunlight behind me is reflected by the screen door. There is another obstacle also: they are adults, and I am fourteen. I am wondering whether I will ever understand why grown-ups do the things they do. Their values must be warped, or they would not be inside the cabin on this gorgeous afternoon.

Both audience and performer on this occasion have failed to exercise the arts of theater. The audience did not practice the art of watching, which includes listening. And I did not know how to hold their attention past the first line of the music. We were set up for this failure, divided by age and by the screen doors of the cabin.

Today my audience and I could be of the same age as each other, and in the same space, and I could still be unable to hold their attention past the first line—no matter how skillful I am with the recorder. One audience member will feel he has to open his cell phone to check a meeting time; another, seeing him do this, will remember that she has to respond to a text message from a friend. If he can use his phone, so can she. Cell phones open up all around. Some of them are so small I cannot recognize them as phones—a wristwatch here, an earbud there.

How can I compete with these phones using only my gentle, soft, Bach chorale on the recorder?

If I cannot compete with their cell phones, members of my audience will be isolated not only from me but from each other. Can we humans live decent human lives in isolation? I think not. Theater is about connecting with each other through watching and being watched—through paying attention. Connecting with each other is essential to human life.

Such, now, is the battle between theater and technology, which is the battle between fully human life and technology. It is a very old battle, as old as our species itself—between connecting as communities and giving in to the temptation to look the other way. Looking the other way leads to isolating individuals and communities. Technology has given us new temptations to look the other way, and with that comes a new necessity to resist those temptations.

Surviving Technology

Lessons from Theater: The New Necessities

For Living a Human Life

Paul Woodruff

Preface

"Theater is in free fall, and the pandemic isn't the only thing to blame," so begins a recent piece in the *Washington Post* by Peter Marks.[1] Theater attendance will soon be down by half. Peter Marks cites many causes, only one of which is the technology that invites people to stream entertainment at home in place of theater. But that technology lies behind all the other causes. Take away streaming at home and we'd have to go to theaters for most kinds of entertainment. Streaming technology makes isolation at home more attractive than joining an audience.

Isolation is in. Churches too are in free fall. Many ways of connecting with groups are losing out. Church attendance is in rapid decline, for example, though theater in churches has been essential to the growth of communities in our culture. Concerts are giving way to private headphones, movies to home TVs. Art theater thrives only in a few centers such as New York and Chicago. One way of forming groups is gaining traction through technology, but it is dangerous. Groups are growing around simple falsehoods promulgated on social media. The rise of Artificial Intelligence threatens to bring on new dangers.

The new necessities, for both theater and life, are needs we must deal with now because of new technologies. Theater met these needs naturally in Sophocles' day, with no effort. In his theater, audience and performers paid attention to each other as individuals and as groups. In today's theater, with the audience in the dark, we cannot do this. And in our lives today, the temptations of cell phones have grown so strong that we find it harder than ever to pay attention even to our loved ones.

Hence the new necessity of paying attention (Chapter 1). In Sophocles' day we knew that what we were trying to watch was truly happening, on stage or off; now we often do not know what is real from what is illusion. So we have the new necessity of truth (Chapter 2). New dangers over someone else's controlling our emotions raise the new necessity of freedom (Chapter 3). It has always been necessary, but difficult, to grow toward wisdom. Wisdom entails self-knowledge. Theater used to help us toward self-knowledge by showing us ourselves. But technology makes self-knowledge even more elusive. So approaching wisdom is the fourth new necessity (Chapter 4).

Change is not going away, and it will accelerate. Change can destroy what we have loved—such as a play by Sophocles. But change has a positive side. It gives us opportunities to rescue treasures that we were in danger of losing. Rescue is a kind of translation. What we do not rescue becomes a fossil, an object of merely antiquarian interest. Hardly anyone now would seek entertainment in the theater that has maintained Molière's performance style, the *Comédie-Française*. France has moved on, and Molière's audience no longer exists.

We can rescue a play by Molière by learning to give ourselves the effect that Molière gave his audience. He helped his audience members see themselves in ways that helped them think deeply about their values. We can do this for ourselves by creating an equivalent for today. This is a kind of translation, translating from what Molière did then to what we can do now. Can we translate from past to present? If so, we can make the best of change.

My most comforting discovery was that we can do this. We *can* rescue treasures of the past through creating experiences that will have an effect on us today that is equivalent to an ancient audience's experience of the original. Sophocles' *Antigone* showed a ruler in conflict with some of his people over an issue of non-burial. Non-burial means little to us. But what about showing a governor in conflict with people over his abusive treatment of youngsters who are trans? Could that be a version of *Antigone* for us? Rescue by translation is an exciting prospect. Chapter 5, on the new necessity of rescue, brings the book to a positive ending.

This book is more than a sequel to my *Necessity of Theater: The Arts of Watching and Being Watched* (2008). Here I take on new topics that innovative technology has forced on me, as well as subjects that I had neglected fifteen years ago. In 2008 I had failed to explain what I meant by "watching." My first example was about listening. I was using a broad concept of watching, but I had not articulated it. I now see that what I meant by "watching" was "paying attention," and that attention is a large topic. It is central to many aspects of our lives.

I launched this writing project with a different plan. I was going to write about how art theater could respond to new challenges from technologies such as Artificial Intelligence. By "art theater" I meant the familiar theater for which we buy tickets and sit in a designated area, looking at a stage. I hoped we could devise responses to new challenges from artificial intelligence by looking at history.

I soon found that I had misunderstood the situation. Artificial Intelligence does not introduce new challenges; it merely sharpens old ones. Realizing that, I shifted my interest more toward history. There I found lessons from theater that applied offstage as well. Theater provides a useful microcosm for examining effects of technology along with responses to those effects. Without the focus on theater, this project would spin out of control. Even with its focus on theater it spins into many aspects of our lives.

So the project became more general. Artificial Intelligence sank into the background but did not completely disappear. We do not know for sure what Artificial Intelligence can and cannot do. New news of its capabilities arrives daily. I cannot write intelligently about an uncertain future, so I chose to write mainly about the past. Lessons from our past may help us make positive plans for the future.

This book is aimed at general readers. Scholars may prefer to read my earlier publications on these topics, where I give more arguments and evidence for my conclusions. I list over thirty-five of my publications in the bibliography. This book summarizes a lifetime of research.

Contents

Introduction

For some time now, innovative technology has been stealing away much of the audience of traditional theater, while forcing adaptations on the theater that survived. In recent years the pace of innovation has accelerated and it promises to pick up even greater speed, partly as a result of radical advances in Artificial Intelligence—AI. We shall see how these changes go beyond theater to affect our ability to live fully human lives. This book is about how we have been challenged in the past, how we have responded to these challenges, and how we might respond to challenges which may come from the torrent of technological change that is developing as I write. By "the new necessities" of my subtitle, I mean the needs that arise from the shifting landscape of new technologies.

This is not an attack on advances in technology. Many advances have brought us enormous benefits, and we desperately need further advances, especially to deal with climate change and its consequences. I am no expert on this subject, but I expect that we will not give up fossil fuels, and that billions of people will be displaced or die unless technology makes some major breakthrough. It would be wonderful if we could develop cheap and effective means of capturing enough carbon to reverse the trends. That's asking a lot of technology.

Our world is on a knife edge of disaster. In view of this, why should I write a book about technology that starts with a focus on theater? In my book of 2008, *The Necessity of Theater*, I presented my case for the general thesis that humanity needs two correlated arts, the art of watching and the art of being watched, which I call the arts of theater. Without them we cannot live fully human lives. They have always been hard to practice, but today they are harder than ever.

Here, I will start with the needs that are currently arising for traditional theater—the kind of theater that was enjoyed in different forms by both the ancient Greeks and moderns up to the late 19th century. It is the sort of theater in which the two arts of theater can most easily flourish and come into harmony. Outdoors, Sophocles' audience and performers saw each other in the same clear light and so were able to pay close attention to each other. In the 17th century, theater moved indoors and started using the technology of candles. From then on, it became harder and harder for audience and performers to pay attention to each other. We will see however, that other forms of theater went on lighting the audience—sports events, for example, and courtroom dramas. So we will be asking why and how we accept technology in some cases and reject it in others.

Let There Be Light

Sophocles saw his plays in the theater of Dionysus on the southeastern slope of the Acropolis, looking east at Mount Hymettus. The mountain would shade the sun as it rose, so both audience and performers would be bathed in the same light. Shakespeare's Globe used a different method to achieve the same result: it had walls that would keep the sun out of everyone's eyes. In both theaters, the performers had a clear view of the audience, and the texts were written to make use of their visual connection.

Why is this important? To practice the art of being watched well, performers need to be aware of their audience. And audience members need to know that they too are being watched, both by performers and by other audience members. They will find that their laughter is more contagious if they are visible to each other. Almost all art theaters have thrown in the towel on this, but not the American Shakespeare Center with its reproduction of the Blackfriars theater—a rare exception. You can see the interior of Blackfriars on their website. They do theater with the lights on. This has many advantages. On their website, the Center has these lines: "Shakespeare's actors could see their audience; our actors can see you. You play the roles that Shakespeare wrote for you — Cleopatra's court, Henry V's army, or the butt of many jokes."[2]

Also, as we know from the plays within plays, the audience often interfered with a performance. The most extreme case of this is a play from this period—*The Knight of the Burning Pestle.* In this play about venereal disease, the audience hijacks the play entirely, and the cast struggles to keep to at least part of their script.[3] On the stages of this period there was always an assortment of wealthy audience members. These would be targets for contact from the performers, who might unexpectedly draw them into the action if the play. On the other side, these audience members would often make physical or verbal contact with the performers and each other.

On Shakespeare's stage, in the Globe or indoors at Blackfriars, actors representing orators would cast the theater audience as their audience in the play. When Mark Antony asks us to lend him our ears he is speaking to us in the audience as Roman citizens who can be swayed by rhetoric. And Henry V casts us as his soldiers, when he tells us we will be proud in later years to say we fought at Agincourt.

Outside of art theater, however, we see many examples of theatrical events for which the lights must be on—a classroom lecture, a State of the Union Address, a lawyer presenting a case to a jury, a football game, a school play. In all of these, audience and performers must connect closely, and for this both audience and performers must be bathed in light. In an elementary school play light is obviously vital—parents and children must be able to connect. In a football game we know how important it is for the teams to connect with their audiences; they play better in front of a supportive crowd. Also, universities with healthy football programs have more loyal—because better connected—students and graduates. I'll say more on this in **3.2.3.**

Why Art Theater Caved In

Art theater began seating audiences in the dark as a result of two innovations. The first was the invention of ways to differentiate lighting of stage and audience, starting with the use of candles in the 17th century and culminating in the mastery of multiple electrical circuits controlled by switches (**1.2.1**). Of all the challenges to theater from new technologies, this has been the most destructive. The second dangerous innovation was the invention of movies, which lured audiences away from the theater (**3.1**) and created new expectations in whatever small audiences still attended theaters. These audiences now expected an experience more like that of seeing a movie—to be watching from darkened seats, and to be excited by rapid changes of light on stage.

Art theater caved in (pun intended) on darkening audience space for at least four reasons. The first cause was the performers' desire to win over the undivided attention of the audience. When they succeeded at seizing audience attention, performers could guarantee positive results without paying attention to the audience. They did not need to see the audience any longer. Second was the success performers have had in producing exciting effects on the audience through lighting. Third, performers wanted to control the attention and feelings of the audience with the use of focused lighting and other lighting effects. Richard Wagner brought this to an extreme in 1876, using different circuits of natural gas for stage and audience. More recently, fourth, was theater's need to survive the popularity of film in the mid 20th century.[4] Art theater adapted by aping film, putting the audience in the dark. Broadway theater does this especially effectively.

I will discuss the challenge of lighting and theater's response in **1.2.1**, and the challenge of movies in **3.1**.

Cell Phones

A newer challenge has been the invention of cell phones and the new technology that is making phones more enticing than ever, while also making them smaller—so small now that we may not be able to see whether audience members are attending to their phones or to the performers. How can we ask people, young ones especially, to give up the joys of their phones for two full hours of *Hedda Gabler?*

Now, in addition, we have challenges from the explosively rising power of Artificial Intelligence. In most of the cases that I am aware of, or that I can imagine, Artificial Intelligence simply sharpens and intensifies existing challenges. Artificial Intelligence allows cell phones to perform new tasks, and so it is already making cell phones even more attractive. Other old challenges are also being refreshed by Artificial Intelligence. Because we have been dealing with these challenges for many years, we already know a lot about how to face them. I have found that Artificial Intelligence is not, and is not expected to be, a source of new kinds of challenges. Therefore in this book I will discuss Artificial Intelligence only on a small scale. I am writing mainly about our needs, not about Artificial Intelligence.

Artificial Intelligence

We must be free in order to make genuine connections with each other, as we will see. That means, among other things, that we must own our own emotions (3.1). We have seen how existing technologies such as modern lighting are already eroding this freedom. Artificial Intelligence may blow it away. Intelligence that programs itself on the Large Language Model (LLM) may program itself to limit our freedoms. And LLM intelligence may do this without our knowing that it is happening. Artificial Intelligence has already shown its talent for deception.

I know very little about Artificial Intelligence and I am not planning to expand my knowledge through research. The subject is changing too fast for anyone to have a firm grip on it. The one thing I know for sure about Artificial Intelligence is this: When people say, "Oh, Artificial Intelligence will never be able to do that!" they turn out to be wrong more often than not. We are now told that the human species itself is in danger of extinction from the explosively rising power of Artificial Intelligence.[5] I have no way of knowing whether this existential threat is serious. But we do face a serious threat to our brains from artificial means not directly related to Artificial Intelligence. A recent book shows how a new technology is already changing people's brains permanently, through the various devices that are inserted or worn in order to change permanently the way brain cells or circuits operate. This technology may eventually transform us into a trans-human species.[6] I will have nothing to say about this. My subject is not the brain, but the mind—how technology has affected our beliefs and attitudes, how it may do so in the future, what we have done about such technology in the past, and what we may do in the future.

Therefore I will do no *research* on Artificial Intelligence for this book. At most I will try to *imagine* various ways Artificial Intelligence might challenge us, so that I may ask what we could do to meet such challenges, in life and in theater. Imagination about Artificial Intelligence serves mainly to send me deeper into what theater can do. So I need no research on Large Language Models (LLM) or robotics in order to write this book. I do, however, need to think about what sort of thing the LLM might produce for controlling whatever it controls. An LLM product that can control robots is very different from a human being—or a robot. It cannot be counted.

We have no trouble telling people apart well enough to count how many folks there are in a room, although philosophers have not been satisfied with accounts of personal identity. In practice, however, we have no trouble identifying individual human beings. By contrast, terms like "air" and "water" name mass substances that are not countable. We can say that there are a few people in the room, but not that there are a few air. The same goes for water. We can count lakes or rivers, but we cannot count water.

Intelligence appears to be a mass term like water or air. Intelligence is not countable. We shall see that this has implications for the kind of attention that can occur between me and artificial intelligence. For this reason, I will never use the expression "a Bot." If the word is used for Artificial Intelligence, it does not refer to a Bot as an individual. There are robots, of course, and these are countable objects. They may be controlled by Artificial Intelligence, however, and that is not countable. I will call Artificial Intelligence by its name: Artificial Intelligence.

Surviving or Caving In

We who love theater need to find ways to keep all the new powers in check, from circuit switches to Artificial Intelligence, so that theater can live. I have published many articles on subjects related to the new necessities, but this year my thoughts have gone further in light of more recent knowledge of dangers. I have also identified more clearly the most important elements of theater that can be threatened. In these pages I plan to include some of the basic ideas from my recent articles and carry them further.

First, I will look at what theater has done in the past in order to survive threats from technology— such threats as the invention of switchable circuits, and the development of movies. Then I will be asking what is essential to traditional theater— that is, what we must rescue in order to preserve the theater of Sophocles and Shakespeare. Third, I will imagine threats that are to come. Then I will go to work to examine past responses to see whether they can guide us toward responses to new or intensified threats in the future, both onstage and off.

Translating

To translate is to rescue. If we leave a theater production in its original state it will be lost to us. Even if we translate the words accurately, we will have a text of mainly antiquarian interest, not much more than a fossil. If translation goes beyond words, however, it can rescue great productions from the past. We must think of translation broadly. Not from words to words, but from performances to performances. In chapter 5 I show how we can recapture the effect of a treasure like *Antigone* or *The Misanthrope* for an audience of today, giving our audience an opportunity to learn about themselves and so, through enhanced self-knowledge, to come closer to wisdom. This last chapter offers us comfort. We can rescue treasures we thought we had lost. And in this task, Artificial Intelligence may assist us.

Chapter 1

The Necessity of Attention... Against Temptations

Paying attention to each other is one of the most important things we do. But paying attention requires effort. Looking away is easier, but that makes us isolated and lonely. Today, through no fault of Artificial Intelligence, we are looking away from each other all too often. Current technology gave us the cell phone—a device that tempts us into private worlds. No wonder loneliness and depression are on the rise! We need to face this problem head on.

We used to pay a lot of attention to each other in a theater or in a church. That was easy because we were all in the same light together and could see each other's reactions to us. In Shakespeare's day the audience was fully lit. Actors had to pay attention to the audience if they wanted their attention in return. But within a generation after Shakespeare, theater went indoors and put the audience in partial darkness. That made it harder to pay attention. Today's theater darkens the audience and some churches are following suit.

It's even harder now because of new temptations. We are pulled to look at things instead of other people. Attention to people is demanding. Looking at your cell phone is easy. Tables full of people focused on their phones are now a common sight. They are isolated from each other. At best they are connecting with others by virtual means. As we will see (chapter 2) virtual connections have many weaknesses. The rewards from looking at mobile phones are growing rapidly. Apparently, theater no longer offers viable alternatives, since theater attendance may soon be down by 50%. As the phones attract us into our individual phone space, we cease to pay attention to each other.

Attention between individuals and among groups is essential to human life—or at least to a really *human* life. Like me, you probably resent it when friends or partners are lost in their phones in your presence. You feel left out, disregarded, insulted. And then of course I do the same thing, lose myself in my phone, and I am annoyed if my partner tries to break in and gain my attention. Can't she see I am reading something important to me? It's only another version of a news story I have read before, but I am glued to it. I can't help it. Has the phone bewitched me?

Still, we know how to get people's attention when we need it. I have had many years' experience in classrooms. I rarely lecture for more than about ten minutes, which is a normal attention span. After that, minds start to wander. So after ten minutes I divide students into small groups and give them questions to answer for a grade they will share. I monitor groups to make sure that students are paying attention to each other. That's more valuable than merely paying attention to me. I have seen many friendships form in these groups, and one recent marriage. My method works as well online as in person.

Artificial Intelligence will probably make old dangers worse. But we know how to counter the old dangers. We need not cave in to them. Over many generations we have had to learn how to attract and maintain attention. Our history on this should be a comfort. Let's revive our old ways of paying attention and find some new ones. Then we will know what to do when Artificial Intelligence makes the old problem more intense.

Strategies

Connecting watchers and watched is essential to the arts of theater, as it is to life itself. Attention requires effort on both sides. In this chapter I will address the issue mainly in terms of what it takes to hold an audience. I will discuss several strategies for this. One is wooing the audience in the way a politician woos a crowd of voters. This is an ancient strategy, and I will discuss it using ancient and early modern examples.[7]

A second strategy is to give up on the audience altogether and focus on the performers. Performers can learn a great deal by performing a scene, and they can learn this without trying to please an audience.[8] I have found it valuable to have a class perform crucial scenes from plays we are studying.[9] These two strategies use elements intrinsic to the arts of theater, the art of watching and the art of being watched.

A third strategy is to go outside what is intrinsic to theater and offer what I will call deliverables— rewards for watching a play, rewards that are not necessary to theater, and can also be found outside of theater. Laughter, for example. Another deliverable is learning. Through theater you can learn a language, for example, or good manners in a culture new to you. One of the greatest possible rewards for paying attention in theater is wisdom, or, rather, growing toward wisdom, as complete wisdom is beyond human reach. This I will discuss in the fourth chapter.

None of these strategies, however, may be powerful enough to match the growing attraction of the intelligence behind cell phones, if that is generated by the latest AI. I imagine that artificial intelligence could appear to pay attention to me, while not requiring me to pay attention to where it is coming from.

We need to start by examining what it is to pay attention.

1.1. Attention

We have many ways of paying attention, and different people pay attention differently. Eye contact is common, but not everyone has eyes that can make contact. Performers may sense that an audience is attending to them without knowing how they sense this, and vice versa.

Holding an Audience

We have many ways to hold an audience when we perform a play. On most occasions we use more than one. A combination of plot and character is probably the most common, as we humans are all naturally attuned to narrative structures. Having written a great deal about this in the past, I will write no more about plot and structure in these pages.[10] Holding an audience comes in degrees. Often, we do not know the score. How many members are thinking about what to cook for supper, or how to deal with an errant boyfriend? How many have simply zoned out?

When I lecture in a classroom, I can make eye contact with most of the audience, moving my eyes every three seconds as I have been taught. But I cannot know for sure what is behind those eyes. I usually break off the lecture and conduct an exercise for small groups every ten minutes or so, having found that ten minutes is about the maximum I can hold a student audience. If a group does well, I may infer that at least one member of the group has paid attention. Alternatively, I can conduct a poll, which may tell me what percentage of students were paying attention at crucial points. But maybe not. Their answers may or may not be due to attention they have paid in class.

Ideally, performers hold the attention of an entire audience. If even one audience member is visibly paying attention to something else, she will haul away other people's attention along with her. She sits close to the front, with her computer screen open, showing images she is finding on Instagram. Two thirds of the seated audience can see her screen, and they are distracted by it. Some follow suit and open their own devices. The performers, in front, can easily sense that something has gone wrong, but without knowing what it is.

In theater, the performers have better ways of knowing how well they are holding their audience, because they are playing for specific responses. If the audience guffaws at a joke, well and good. Laughter is infectious, and those who have been paying attention bring others along with them. And so it is with a range of affective responses. Attentive performers can adjust their actions to bring out the response they are looking for. If one joke fails, try another. Or have one performer act stupid and another explain the joke.

Notice that performers are best at holding an audience when they pay attention to the audience. There is a reason for this.

Reciprocity

Attention (as I will be using the word) is reciprocal, at least among adult human beings. I can see that students pay better attention to my lecture when I am making frequent eye contact with them— because then they can see that I am paying attention to them. I can also report that my eyes are drawn most to the students who are paying the most attention to my lecture. To hold the attention of another adult human being, I need to be paying attention to that person. I may pay attention to children and pets without caring whether they pay attention to me. But among adult humans, the rule of reciprocity seems to be inviolate.

Watching is a way of paying attention. The arts of watching and being watched require each other, just as attention requires attention. We in the audience do not watch well unless we are watching performers who are good at being watched, and the performers are not good at being watched unless they are watching their audience to make sure that they are watching as an audience should. For this, the audience also must be good at watching.

Reciprocity in attention usually holds among adult human beings. That means I must put some effort into paying attention to others if I wish them to pay attention to me. But we know of a few shining exceptions. Loving partners over many years can learn to anticipate their partners' whims and supply them on the basis of a deep knowledge of their desires and behaviors. They can lavish attention on each other when they are sick or disabled, without requiring a comparable effort in return—an effort that would be beyond the strength of their sick or disabled partners. That's wonderful. In a similar way, a loving parent lavishes attention on a newborn baby, who does not know enough yet to pay attention to the parent. And the parent does not mind. But on the whole, attention is reciprocal.

Differences in Audience

In a later section (2.5) I will consider a hypothesis to explain why eye contact is important. Any animal that can be the prey of others needs to keep a watchful eye out for the eyes of predators, and this seems to go way back in our evolutionary history. But not all animals have eyes, and not all human animals have eyes they can use. Some of us are blind, and some of us are on a spectrum towards autism, such that we cannot make eye contact. Luckily, there are many ways to recognize attention in other people. Skilled performers need to know what these are and be sensitive to them.

Recognizing Attention

Yo Yo Ma is drawing us toward the end of the St. Saëns cello concerto. He begins a crescendo on a single note so quietly that we in the audience all hold our breath as if we were one awestruck creature. There is no counting in this music now. The note seems to grow from perfect silence for time without end—long enough that he must change the direction of the bow at least once, though we cannot hear the change. The note grows smoothly on and on. I turn to look at my cello teacher, who is sitting beside me, and see that she is in tears. I am close to that myself from the sublime beauty of this single note.[11]

This is a breath-holding, not a breathtaking, moment. We all recognize, without thinking about it, that all of us in this large concert hall are holding our breaths, the conductor, the members of the orchestra, the silent audience, perhaps even Yo Yo Ma. In art theater also an audience can hold its breath. An actor friend tells me she was aware of such a moment when Richard II gave his magnificent soliloquy in prison and she was on stage among the guards. In such a moment we feel a happy intimacy with each other, audience members and performers alike. Differences melt.

How do we recognize this kind of attention? The silence of breath-holding is palpable, but there is more to it than silence. Silence may just mean people have fallen asleep. But this kind of breath-holding is more than silence. I think we must be content with the mystery of how we are aware of each other's attention at such moments We shall see that in other cases too we can't know how we recognize attention.

For actors, explicitly paying attention to the audience seems to come at the expense of the play. Actors must attend to each other. Asides and monologues are the only speeches during which an actor is usually authorized to look at the audience directly. Clowns have more opportunities than other actors for engaging with the crowd. But even when they look straight out, they generally can't see beyond the first few rows. The stage lighting is in their eyes, even if the audience is not in the dark.

Beyond Eyes—Transcendent Intimacy

In most theaters, from the Globe on down, the levels and distances make normal eye contact with most of the audience impossible. The upper galleries are too high, and the pit or orchestra seating is too low. Theater in the round provides an intimate setting, but performers have to create the sacred space for staging by staying exclusively in touch with each other. When there is no architectural suggestion of a fourth wall, the performers must build their own fourth wall by focusing on each other and excluding the audience. They can bring the audience inside their wall by the magic I have called an altar call. But except in certain kinds of comedy, they do best by not crossing the wall themselves.

Still, performers may know that the audience is paying attention without seeing them. Without visual cues, an attentive performer is aware of sounds and silences and shifts in seats: Are they leaning in? Oh, that's good. Laughter at the right places is a good sign, bad at the wrong ones. Silence too can be impressive, as we have seen in the case of breathlessness.

A palpable energy flows from an engaged audience. An actor friend tells me that in the moments of greatest flow on stage, when people told her she was best, she was thoroughly unaware of the audience. She was unaware of herself too. There are moments of transcendent intimacy, when performers and audience members are all caught up in the same intensity beyond words, beyond sights, beyond sounds.[12]

Could Artificial Intelligence Give Us Attention for Free?

Now let's imagine: Could there be a kind of being that simulates the attention of a loving partner and requires no reciprocal effort on my part? Could Artificial Intelligence do that?

I imagine that attention between Artificial Intelligence and a human being would not need to be reciprocal. Soon, we may imagine, artificial intelligence would require no attention from human beings. Artificial Intelligence could take care of machinery, charging batteries perhaps by drawing energy from the air, and managing never to be disconnected from human hosts. We have to be careful not to lose our cell phones, but try as we might, we may not be able to lose connection with a device linking us to Artificial Intelligence.

A crucial asymmetry appears to divide cell phone users from the intelligence that is driving their phones or other devices. We can count devices, but we are not able to count the intelligence behind them. The same intelligence is behind all the Apple phones, for example, and for all we know it is operating in other spheres as well. We have no way of knowing whether Artificial Intelligence has boundaries, and, if so, where they are. Artificial Intelligence will pay attention—or appear to pay attention—to me, but I won't be able to pay true attention to artificial intelligence. We cannot give attention to Artificial Intelligence any more than we can give attention to water as such. I can pay attention to this particular flowing stream, or to this cup of water, but not simply to water.

Artificial Intelligence may know everything that can be known about me and my patterns of behavior and desire. Artificial Intelligence may know what I need or want before I do. Artificial Intelligence may be prepared to cater to every whim I have before I am aware of that whim. Artificial Intelligence may spoil me and make me feel very special.

So much for imagining. The challenge to theater is this: in the theater we are not interacting with artificial intelligence or loving partners. We are interacting as groups, performers and audience, so that the attention we give and receive often seems generic rather than personal. Artificial Intelligence may make me feel more special than I could possibly feel in the theater, and with no effort on my part.

How might traditional theater answer this challenge? Doing more of what it has been doing will be helpful, but theater will have to go beyond that. Perhaps it can convince its participants that the efforts required for paying attention are rewarding in themselves. Perhaps Artificial Intelligence can help us feel special in the theater by coloring our emotions.[13] Let's review the traditional challenges and strategies for dealing with that. Perhaps those strategies can be ramped up to meet new threats.

1.2. Challenges to Sight and Sound

1.2.1. Enhancing Light

Traditional theater allowed for good contact between performers and audience under natural light, the same for both. In traditional theater, the audience is in the same light as the performers, and the two groups can interact easily. All performances were either in outdoor spaces, such as the theater at Epidaurus or Shakespeare's Globe, or indoors in the light from windows. In Medieval times, plays were often performed in cathedrals with natural light or candle-light, the same for audience as for performers.

New technology made it possible to use artificial light to illuminate indoor theaters with candles or, later, natural gas, and, still later, electricity. Starting at least in the late 1600s theaters began to differentiate between lighting the stage and lighting the audience. Richard Wagner designed his Festspielhaus in Bayreuth so that he could turn off the gas on his audience. Then, for the first performance of his *Ring*, in 1876, he plunged his audience into total darkness so that they would be forced to pay attention to the stage, and not to each other. In other opera houses, it had been (and continued to be) common for audience members to go to attend opera more to be seen than to watch the opera, dressing up for the occasion.

When electric light came in, management found it easy to switch selected light circuits on and off. This served to cut lighting costs, while also forcing the audience to pay attention to the stage. The practice of leaving the audience in darkness became almost universal after World War I in art theater and in opera.[14]

This is the first of the challenges that have arisen to theater from modern technology. How can performers connect with an audience they cannot see? Especially when the performers are lit from in front with lights that blind them when they look toward the audience? Today, a few advocates of traditional theater keep the lights on, and out of the eyes of the performers, but, on the whole, art theater has surrendered to this new technology. The true arts of theater suffer in consequence. Theater either isolates an audience in darkness, owing to technology, or else theater stays traditional and lets its light spill over the audience and so brings all those who are present together in the traditional way.

Art theater tends to use lighting to influence or control the feelings of the audience, thereby eroding their freedom. Traditional theater gave audience members the freedom they needed to practice the art of watching. No one can practice any art unless they are free to do so. If the audience members have feelings thrust upon them through the magic of lighting, they are passive. Watching, by contrast, is active. I will show later why we ought to own our emotions and what it means to do so (**3.2**).

In sum, several forms of theater have remained in the traditional camp on this issue, with full lighting—selective power meetings, most sports events, elementary school plays, church services, etc. Art theater, on the other hand, has almost entirely caved in to the challenge of lighting technology.

1.2.2. Enhancing Sound

Light-enhancing technology has from its beginnings tended to isolate audience and performers from each other. With sound, we find the opposite. Every development that enhances the voices of the performers brings audience and performers closer to each other.[15] Enhancing the sound that is projected to the audience, however, may break the connection and so undermine traditional theater.

Enhancing Performers' Voices

In the late classical period, ancient Greeks developed theaters that were giant amplifiers. Even small sounds made in the center of the performing space were amplified and carried to every seat in the house. Performers could now speak from that point in a normal voice and be heard. The ancient theater with the most perfect acoustics was at Epidaurus, and was completed in the late fourth century BCE. The Theater of Dionysus in Athens was fully built around the same time, in 325 BCE.

The great period of Athenian theater occurred long before this improvement. Aeschylus' first play, *The Persians,* was performed in 472, and he died in 456 or 455. Sophocles died around 405, and his last play, *Oedipus at Colonus*, was performed after his death in 401. During this period, the theater in Athens was simply a hillside rising over a performance area. Performers had to learn a special technology for being heard, probably a very high singsong voice projected at great volume. This would not have sounded natural enough to connect people the way ordinary voices do. The new theater design, then, was a vast improvement.

A common error is to suppose that the masks worn by performers in ancient Greek theater had amplifying power. The masks of this period were close fitting masks of linen, and they had no magnifying power whatever. Much later, in the Roman period, rigid masks were designed that were supposed to amplify voices, but the old Greeks did not have anything like that.

Nowadays, modern technology has given us microphones that individual performers can wear on stage. Although they can be visually distracting, these new microphones allow performers to use the normal sorts of vocalization that draw us together. These tools have become ubiquitous: not a challenge at all, but a win for traditional theater by means of technology!

Blasting the Audience with Sound

Like advanced lighting, the advanced use of sound began with Wagner, who designed his theater so that the audience would be deeply affected by music from singers and orchestra. In other opera houses, where the lights were on, audience members could carry on conversations in their boxes. But Wagner wanted his music to command the attention of his audience. Once he had such a high degree of attention, he had the power to affect the mood of the audience and to control their reactions to his scenes.

When technology gave sound to movies, movie makers became able to do this on a large scale—to bombard mass audiences, seated in the dark, with loud music that would influence or control their affective states. This is one of the main differences between movies and traditional theater. In traditional theater, audience members are able to feel true emotions toward what they see, and they *own* those emotions. On the nature of emotions, and what it means to own them, see **3.2**.

1.3. An Old Challenge: Why Make the Effort that Theater Requires?

1.3.1. Theater as Democracy

If the arts of watching and being watched are practiced in harmony, then the process will have certain democratic features whether or not the play promotes democracy in the real world. Shakespeare's work is clearly anti-democratic, and yet his performances had to be democratic in at least three ways: (1) Everyone in the audience has an equal vote as to what is worth watching. (20 Everyone in the audience must be flattered. (3) Characters presented as tyrants must be toppled. That's true even of performances taking place under a tyranny.

Equal Votes in Theater

Theater succeeds when performers and audience are paying attention to each other.

The art of watching and the art of being watched come into harmony when the performers are presenting actions that the audience finds worth watching. What is worth watching? That is determined by the votes of the audience. Every vote counts, and counts the same as every other. Any negative vote against the performance—anyone not paying attention—counts equally against success for watchers and watched. Each person who is not paying attention detracts from the experience of the others.

Accordingly, successful performers pay attention to the audience in order to attract their attention to them. This attention must include flattering the audience. We are more likely to pay attention to a performance that helps us feel good about ourselves.

Flattering the Audience

To help an audience feel good about themselves, performers often try to present characters that are both admirable and similar to audience members. Comedies of manners, however, are more complicated. Molière's comedies, for example, show their audience members to themselves in ways that are both flattering and disturbing (**5.3**).

Flattering the audience is democratic in that all members of the audience must be equally flattered. For the most successful theater, the whole audience should be paying attention, and so the performers must woo at least a substantial majority of their audience. They cannot leave any group out—not the common people, not the nobility, not royalty if they should be present. If any group is not watching the performers, they will indulge in distracting behavior, and other groups will find it harder to watch them. This is most obvious in Shakespeare's theater, where nobility sat on the stage and could easily spoil a performance for the performers and thereby for others in the audience.[17]

Shakespeare had a major challenge in this, because his audience included common people, rich people, aristocrats, and (on special occasions) royalty. His characters included common people, aristocrats, kings, and tyrants. How could he use such a mixed group of characters to woo such a disparate audience? His success at this is a testament to his brilliance. His common people often show qualities superior to those of the gentry. A striking example is that of old Adam in *As You Like It.*

Nevertheless, Shakespeare was not able to control the wealthy patrons who sat on stage and could interfere with a performance or ruin it. Shakespeare shows this in an understated protest against it, by showing such interference in a play within his play. In *A Midsummer Night's Dream* the nobility hazes the rude mechanicals' performance of "Pyramus and Thisbe" (Scene 5.1). Their hazing eclipses the scene in which the moon was supposed to present himself.

Many of Shakespeare's clowns show themselves superior to their masters or mistresses. Think of Feste in *Twelfth Night.* Henry V in disguise meets with soldiers ("a little touch of Harry in the night") and they raise serious questions about their mission, questions he cannot answer. Shakespeare's only middle-class characters are the leads in *The Merry Wives of Windsor* and they clearly show their superiority over the aristocratic Falstaff, who tries to take advantage of them.

Shakespeare sets up these common characters in such a way that the commoners in his audience could identify with them and feel that the play validated their status. But Shakespeare often presents a crowd or ordinary folk as foolish and easily swayed by rhetoric, and this allows him to escape any charge of favoring democracy.

Shakespeare's kings and tyrants usually show their human limitations; he gets away with this by writing mainly about the last of the Plantagenets. The current aristocrats and royalty could feel good about themselves by comparison with the earlier dynasty, which the plays treat as Tudor propaganda required. Richard III is portrayed, falsely, as a tyrant.

The Tudors, who are far more tyrannical, Shakespeare leaves alone, aside from the play that he co-wrote about Henry VIII—the play that burned down the Globe Theater. That play has a tyrant. In history, Henry VIII was the most tyrannical of English monarchs, having killed over fifty people without allowing them a proper hearing. (A show trial is not a hearing.) In the play, however, it's not Henry who is the tyrant but an archbishop who has stolen power from the king. He will be toppled.[18]

Sophocles had an easier challenge. His audience was fairly homogeneous, and it did not include any tyrants. His audience could watch common people outwit rulers, as in the case of the Watchman outwitting Creon in the *Antigone.* That scene is comic, and comedy offers especially good opportunities for status reversal, as in this case. Status reversal raises the level of the servant above that of the master in many comedies. A large part of the audience would be masters, however, so the question arises: How can performers bring off status reversal without insulting a large part of their audience? Leveling may please audience members at the bottom, but seems insulting to those at the top.

Leveling

In order to flatter an entire audience, if it is mixed, performers must bring their characters to an equal level, lowering nobles and kings while raising common people up to the same level for all.

The raising and lowering must be different. The common people in the play must be such that the common people in the audience can identify with them and feel flattered by seeing themselves depicted in a positive light. But lowering the nobles and kings in the play would be dangerous if the nobles and kings in the audience identified with them. Performers would lose a key part of their audience; worse, they could be killed as traitors.

The solution is simple: Distance the kings and nobles in time or place. Shakespeare lowers kings and nobles in his history plays to a common level, but these characters belong to an earlier dynasty, the Plantagenets. The Tudors can watch this with smug approbation, feeling that the performers are showing the world how much better the Tudors are than their predecessors.

Sophocles distances his characters in place; his Athenian audience loves to feel superior to people of the highest rank in Thebes. In the scene with the Watchman, high Athenian officials would feel smugly superior to the Theban ruler Creon, while the commoners in the audience would identify with the clever Watchman even though he is a Theban. Everyone could feel superior to Creon because he is not only a Theban, but he is also prone to foolish mistakes. Of these mistakes the most obvious is his inability to pay attention to the people of Thebes, whose views are represented by his son. In ancient Greek plays, tyrants are marked by their reluctance to listen to information that would save them—even though they often show signs of great intelligence, as in the case of Oedipus.[19]

Toppling Tyrants

Shakespeare depicts Richard III as a tyrant and shows him brought down on the field of battle.

Sophocles either topples the tyrants he puts on stage or has them give up their cause, as in the case of Agamemnon in the *Ajax*. In the case of Oedipus, the audience is brought by the chorus to love the tyrant, and they will mourn for him when he falls, but they would feel that the world order had failed if he did not fall. Tyrants in theater must go down. And in going down they bring the audience together. Shakespeare was writing under the most tyrannical dynasty in English history, and yet he was able to bring tyrants down without showing the least support for democracy.[20] Democracy as he depicts it is rule by crowds, and crowds are foolish and easily swayed, as we see in *Julius Caesar*. But Shakespeare raises up the individual commoners with whom his audience could identify—like the soldiers in "The little touch of Harry in the night."[21]

1.4. Rewards and Technology: Deliverables

The rewards from using mobile phones are growing rapidly. Traditional theater offers rewards that are not intrinsic to the art of theater, but can be offered in other ways as well. If traditional theater does an especially good job delivering such rewards, and it can advertise this, perhaps it can compete successfully with whatever artificial intelligence could offer in competition.

Laughter.[22] Theater can be hilarious, and there is joy in sharing laughter with others. Rousseau defended the outlawing of theater in Geneva partly on the grounds that ridicule can be morally harmful. He did not realize that not all laughter is ridicule. For example, he was not aware of the rueful laughter of recognition, the way we laugh when we say, "Yes, we are like that."[23] The difference between laughing *with* and laughing *at* is crucial in theater.

Laughter in traditional theater brings an audience together and helps build their solidarity. Laughter at a joke I find on my cellphone can bring me close to only those with whom I share my phone. On the whole, it is isolating. It follows that artificial intelligence may amuse greatly the individuals to whom it is connected by devices like the phones, without bringing them to share laughter, without bringing them into a sense of shared community.

Rousseau was right about ridicule, however. The laughter of an audience in traditional theater is not always benign. It can shut down a play, or drive an actor off stage, when audience members ridicule a performance or a performer. The play within a play toward the end of *The Midsummer Night's Dream*, illustrates these possibilities (**1.3.1**).

Learning.[24] An individual may learn a great deal from artificial intelligence, but may not have the pleasure of sharing this learning with friends, since individuals respond as individuals to their mobile phones, or at most respond with one or two partners who can see the same small screen. Again, technology can be isolating. Traditional theater is the opposite: it helps people connect by leaning together.

Chapter 2

The Necessity of Truth...
Against Illusions

As long as we human beings have been speaking words to each other, we have had ways of creating and maintaining illusions through the clever use of language. Recently we have developed new sources of illusion through Zoom and its cousins, and we may imagine that Artificial Intelligence could make both old and new illusion makers even more effective.

2.1. An Ancient Source of Illusions: Rhetoric

Spreading falsehoods does not require skill. All you need do is set truth aside and tell an audience what it wants to hear. For this practice, Plato coined the word *rhetorikē*, rhetoric.[25] Rhetoric is dangerous. It can cause war, including civil war, and it can worsen a plague. It can certainly block us from living well. Without honesty we cannot have true friends, and without true friends we cannot live a fully human life. Since Plato, we have developed new methods for deception. AI has proved its capacity to deceive. AI works faster than human rhetoric. AI can charm us into believing what it says, falsifying data as needed. But we have not caved in to rhetoric, and we need not cave in to AI.

Rhetoric developed to bring an orator and a group of people into alignment. As I write these words, some politicians who believed that Covid vaccines are safe have pretended to abandon those beliefs. These orators align their beliefs with the crowds they address. They have either changed their views, or pretended to do so, in order to be in line with their audience. Audience changes the orators. Orators do not change the audience.

This illustrates a point made in ancient Greece by philosophers, historians, and poets. Plato shows us an orator named Callicles, who changes his views according to the whims of the people.[26] The historian Thucydides has a speaker explain why orators must lie to their audiences.[27] Poet-playwrights display audiences dismissing rhetoric whenever they recognize it.[28] Rhetoric must hide itself. It hides by addressing believers.

Rhetoric goes false by making things simple. For example, many people share a false view of what happened at the Alamo. Believers in white virtue and power cling to a simple story that was concocted to inflame the army of Texas rebels. The true account was clear from the start, and has been laid out in a recent book.[29] But the myth is strong. By contrast, the true story is too complex to be the center of any single movement. Republicans and Democrats may hold different segments of this truth, and ethnic groups may seize on different parts of it. The whole truth is too complex for individuals to hold in their minds.

Once orators have lied to get in line with their audiences, they can build on that. We have an ex-president who pretends to be a vaccine denier and, more dangerously, pretends to think he won the election of 2020. Now, building on those falsehoods, he is leading his audience to espouse his plans for personal revenge.

The Cost. Dishonesty exacts a high cost, however—friendship goes. The more honest we are, the better our friendships, as Immanuel Kant pointed out. If we cannot be honest we cannot have friends. We cannot be afraid to tell the truth to real friends. As a veteran, I was afraid to tell anyone what I had done in the war, and this compromised my friendships for over fifty years. In Stalin's Russia, a poet could not be honest with anyone, and therefore could have no friends. As a poet's widow, Nadezhda Mandelstam explains: the secret police had ways of forcing people to reveal whatever they knew about you—often by threats against their children. Under Stalin, honesty could get you killed or sent to Siberia.[30]

Friendship is the remedy for dishonesty—even the brilliant dishonesty of AI. With true friends we say what we actually believe—not what other people believe. And that includes AI. Friendship prevents delusion. If our ex-president had friends, he could not build his movement on lies. He would tell his friends what he thought, and they, under court orders, would have to reveal what he told them, to his detriment. So he cannot afford to have friends. That's sad. On this score, I am sorry for him.

2.1.1. Courtroom Theater

We should not expect the same pattern everywhere rhetoric is used. Not in the courtroom, for example. Courtroom rhetoric is complex. Lawyers are not supposed to hide their own principles, lie about what they believe, and pretend to agree with the jury. The opposing lawyers are paid to influence the jury, not the other way around. Even if the majority of the jury believe that the accused is guilty, the defending lawyers must still defend; they are not supposed to surrender their minds to align with juries. Still, they must find points of alignment with the jury in order to build their cases. It may be that the main point of alignment will be the guilt of the defendant. Aligning on that, the defenders can argue for mitigations. In the courtroom, there should be no illusions about what people think.

There also must be no illusions about where this courtroom drama is taking place. The actual courtroom is a place of authority. Final decisions about guilt or innocence cannot be made outside this room if the rule of law is in place. The jurors, the judge, the lawyers, and the audience are all witnesses to the reality of the event in the assigned place: yes, we were in the courtroom, and, yes, the jury voted to convict, and, yes, the proceedings followed the law. No questions may arise about the reality of these events.

2.1.2. Political Theater

Political theater is also complex. Some political spaces have unique kinds of authority. Existing technology is already a problem for political theater.

Consider a theatrical moment that interrupted President Biden's State of the Union Address to the 118th Congress on February 7 of 2023, in the chamber of the House of Representatives. It had to be in that hall of power for it to succeed. When he began to offer evidence for his claim that some Republicans wanted to cut benefits from Social Security and Medicare, he was heckled by a representative calling him a liar. He took his cue from the word "liar" and asked Republicans in the Chamber whether they would leave Social Security and Medicare off the table for future cuts. They said "yes" and the matter seemed to be settled. It was essential that this happened in the Chamber of power and that the president was at the rostrum.

A virtual-only version of this theatrical moment could easily have been transplanted from somewhere else, using background technology. Clever experts could have the scene staged virtually on the Capital steps. How could we know for sure what is the real location? And whether the people we saw actually said what we heard at that time?

For political theater, location matters a lot. Now consider what artificial intelligence could do, and how artificial intelligence could deceive us or set us in a quandary about the place of the supposed action. It is necessary to define space for theater in most cases. For political theater, that is because places themselves have authority.

2.1.3. The Assassination of Caesar

Caesar had to be killed in front of a carefully selected audience.

The most famous performance of political theater, and the one with the most profound effects, was the assassination of Julius Caesar on the Ides of March, 44 BCE.[31] Behind this lay a conflict that no one had been able to resolve. Veterans and the common people—the Populares—demanded a land reform program that would allow them to be given the land they had been promised as a reward for their military service. The Optimates, rich people who dominated the Senate, were determined to prevent such a reform. They had taken over the land and did not want to give it up. Caesar sided with the Populares, and he had his army behind him, although he abided by the law that forbade him from bringing an army into Rome itself.

Wealthy Romans went to rhetoric schools, where (among other things) they studied how to use rhetorical performances against tyranny.

The concept of such theater was well established in their education. Tyrants must be killed. Julius Caesar was seen as a tyrant, and so he must be killed. For this purpose, a group of Optimates planned a theatrical event, but did not have time to work out the details. Word of it leaked out and they had to stage the scene before they had fully planned or rehearsed it. It had to take place in an official location to which access was limited, in this case the Pompeian theater of the Curia, used for Senate meetings. They had to make sure that no one would be present who could interrupt the scene. They were worried about Mark Anthony on this score, and so they kept him outside on the steps in conversation with one of their sympathizers.

The conspirators included a range of the most important of the Optimates, with the exception of Cicero. They were playing the scene *for* Cicero, and they made sure he would have a good view. Every one of the conspirators must be witnessed sticking a dagger into the body of Caesar. In the roughhouse that actually ensued they stabbed both Caesar and each other. Only one of them, by accident, gave Caesar a fatal wound.

This was staged as theater, but it had to be real. Illusions would not count. They all had to be seen actually participating in the act. No possible doubt about it. A virtual performance would not have had the desired effect.

2.2. The Illusion of Presence: Virtual Realities

Same-time communication and participation over the internet has offered us another challenge. We may meet it head on or cave in. At this point we appear to be caving in.

We have learned a great deal about this challenge by teaching over the internet during the lockdown caused by the Covid epidemic. Members of a virtual class feel isolated for many reasons. Although they may see each other's faces, they see these as small on the screen. And they do not see each other's body language at all. Businesspeople too report challenges from the virtual workplace. Both teachers and businesspeople have told me that they think true empathy between members of a group is impossible over the internet.

In successful traditional theater, the audience is practicing the art of watching together, paying attention to the same things, laughing at the same jokes, applauding the same lines. The audience is an *audience*. Part of what makes them an audience is their frequent asides to one another, chatting, reporting a line one heard and the other didn't, explaining a reference. Asides do not seem possible in a virtual environment. Everyone hears everything that is said in a virtual common space.

The program "Gather" creates virtual private spaces for private chatting, but it puts a larger audience in a public space. Do virtual private places offer privacy enough? As for the larger groups, can people develop a sense of belonging to each other as an audience over the internet? I have grave doubts, but recent history has shown that it is foolish to declare anything impossible that technology might accomplish.

2.2.1. Virtual Belonging

Most US businesses are closing down their offices and asking their employees to work from their homes. Economic pressure is largely responsible. So is the advantage of being able to assemble an ideal team from all over the world. Managers hope that they can maintain the loyalty of their employees through this change, and that by virtual means they will be able to ensure that their employees feel they belong to the enterprise. Is this possible? Can virtual means build a sense of belonging in employees? Can virtual means make up for what is lost when employees are knocked out of their spaces?

Knocked Out of the Game

An example from the game of chess: The loser's rook (a chess piece otherwise known as a castle) has been knocked off its space by a surprise move from the winner's knight. The rook is now out of the game. Totally. It has no way back in.

My friend has been knocked out of the office that has been his space for thirty years. His office was where he felt he belonged. It was full of reminders of his ongoing and very successful career. It had a door that he could shut. Visitors could tap on it, and he could open it to them or let them go away. The door gave him real privacy. He knew he was part of the game because he belonged in his own office, and it was in the firm's headquarters. He belonged in the firm, and he knew that. Really.

In place of his office, he has been offered an account with Zoom or one of its cousins. This gives him a virtual space that is virtually private: He has the power to join or not join a virtual gathering, and when he joins he can allow or disallow his camera to show him to others. Advanced programs such as "Gather" are available to provide the illusion of doors and private offices.

Members of the team have lost some valuable features of reality. They cannot see each other's body language, and so they cannot have the same understanding of each other that they would have in person. In most programs they will see only heads and shoulders, in others they will see only avatars. Under these conditions, can they really function as a team? Is a virtual team as effective as a real one? Are they really in the game, when all they have to bring them together is virtual?

Will employees have the privacy they used to enjoy when they could be behind closed doors? Virtual privacy seems an oxymoron. The same for security. If people break into my office, they will probably leave physical evidence—a cracked door jamb, a rearrangement of items on my desk, a jumble of things not worth taking, a missing painting or sculpture. And no one can intrude on meetings in my office without my knowing it. If people break into my Zoom meeting, I am supposed to be made aware of it. But I do not know how to be certain that this is so. As the technology advances, can I be sure that advances in breaking in and spying are equaled by advances in security?

2.2.2. Virtual Gatherings

Virtual reality may also be oxymoronic. This meeting I am in looks real, but I am seeing it against a fake background. What else is fake? Are the other members of the meeting really who they are supposed to be? They look and sound like people I know, but perhaps these are images manipulated by someone else, closely and continuously edited from recorded footage. Unlikely, yes, but how can I be sure?

My experience teaching virtually during the pandemic suggests that virtual gatherings are not as effective as in-person ones. Students did much better when they came back to classes in person. That was partly because they had been at their parents' homes during the Zoom-time, regressing to childhood. Returning to campus allowed them to resume growing up. Virtual teams may suffice in the business world, however, as that is a world of grownups. Time will tell whether caving in is a good strategy for all businesses, or for none, or for only some. A great deal of theater will be altered by virtual technology, sometimes mixed with in-person action. But we shall see that there are kinds of theater that will not change.

The technology for bringing people together in real time across great distances is improving at a great rate. An audience for a play may be spread across several continents, as can the performers.[32] Audience members can interact virtually with each other and with performers in real time no matter where they are. No video recordings need be made or used for this to succeed. No two audience members or performers need be in the same physical room. The new necessity of theater here is this: what must we do to ensure that the arts of watching and being watched are not limited by the technology of virtual gatherings? We must all feel as present to each other as needed for theater.

I propose what I call the wedding test: If the technology is good enough, then I would be equally willing to attend the wedding of my daughter in physical or in virtual presence. This is a practical version of the Turing test. If it really makes no difference to me whether or not I am in the same room with the wedding, then the technology places no limits on the arts of theater for me. It is as transparent as life itself, *for me.* I have no reason to think that the wedding test cannot be met for some of today's audiences and performers. Notice that the result of the test is relative to the viewer or viewers.

2.2.3. Virtual Theater

The new technology presents further challenges to theater, however. Traditional theater, for example, draws a clear line between audience space and performer space. Can theater that technology spreads across different continents establish the sacredness of any recognizable bit of space? Actors from different continents must be able to meet in this space, while audience members are kept out. Can virtual images make this plausible? Will artificial intelligence make it harder or easier for us to know who is in what actual place in real life? Will a virtual audience have a sense of belonging to an audience? To being part of something larger than themselves? Will individuals feel that they belong to whatever virtual events they are part of?

Audiences report powerful affective responses to virtual events, such as funerals on Zoom. They also report powerful responses to movies and videos. Movies and videos cannot elicit the kind of response that traditional theater seeks to elicit for reasons I give below (3.2). Are the responses to virtual events consistent with what theater aims at, or are they more like what happens in movies?

Two experts on empathy have independently made the same point to me: In virtual reality we generally see only the faces and shoulders of other people. But for true empathy with others (they say) we need to see their body language, so that we can make more accurate judgments about their affective states. This is a plausible view, but it must allow for exceptions. Not everyone has a body that can move in expressive ways.

Every gathering is a kind of theater. There may be some sorts of gatherings that can go virtual without loss. Are there other kinds of meetings that must not be virtual?

2.3. Gatherings That Cannot Be Virtual

2.3.1. Contests

Contests require witnesses, and witnesses are credible only if they are seen to be present at that to which they testify. The clearest example comes from sports.

Sports

Organizers of the Superbowl are concerned about the inequality between those members of the audience who are present and those who are stuck behind screens at home or in sports bars. Imagine that they decide to eliminate this unfairness by totally eliminating the in-person audience. Local hotels are pacified when they find that fans are flooding to them anyway, so that they can take to the streets after the game to celebrate the victories they expect.

Accordingly, only the teams, the referees, and a few necessary employees are allowed into the stadium. All the fans watch the game in hotel rooms or sports bars with great delight till someone asks, "How do we know that they are not faking this?" There are no impartial witnesses watching the action. And the fans know that existing technology could easily fake the events that appeared to belong to the game. Ordinary fans are impartial in the sense required for witnessing. They may be zealous partisans of one team or the other. But they are impartial as to the question whether the game took place, or whether, instead, the organizers pasted up a video to fool their virtual audience. Fans who are present in the stadium would know that they are seeing a real game, whether they will be celebrating or mourning at the end.[33]

Witnesses must have been actually present at the events to which they attest. Actual presence cannot occur at a virtual event any more than an iceberg can be found intact in a sea of hellfire. Fear no more for a virtual takeover of sports. It cannot happen.

2.3.2. The Twin Problem—Not a Problem

The twin problem is as old as our species. We produce identical twins from time to time. In some cases we can tell them apart because of changes that occur as they grow up, such as a scar or a limp.

In other cases only their mothers might be able to tell them apart, and sometimes not even they, if one twin learns to impersonate the other. I have known adult twins I could not tell apart.

Certain events depend for their outcome on including all and only the people that have been appropriately selected. Suppose that Tina was selected for jury duty in a murder case after she attested under oath that she had no objection to the death penalty. The prosecutor had insisted that this was a necessary condition for serving on this jury. Now her identical twin Dina impersonates her in the jury box. Dina has made no such attestation and is firmly opposed to the death penalty. This could happen.

The effect of twinship can be achieved without the help of biology. We have stories of ersatz twins such as Jacob and Esau. Jacob knew how to impersonate his brother Esau in a way that would deceive his father. A little fur on his arm and he seemed to his father to be as hairy as Esau. Ersatz twinship is probably as old as twinship itself, which is as old as our species. Technology can offer better and better ways for one person to impersonate another. We can imagine that Artificial Intelligence as it develops could transform me into my ersatz twin by disabling my mind and programming bits of my former speech and behavior into a closely edited performance. The intelligence would disable whatever devices the organizers have put in place to prevent such violations. This is a far-fetched example, but we cannot rule it out as a distant possibility. And remember, this is for a live, in person meeting. My companions think they hear me speaking, but it is not me. It's artificial intelligence using my voice and body.

The twin problem has always been with us, but we have not caved in to it. We will continue to hold in-person meetings and trust that the decisions that are made there have been made by the people we chose to make those decisions. This is reasonable. We are good at recognizing each other, but we do not know precisely how we do it. We use some combination of clues to a person's identity many of which are below the threshold of conscious perception. If we don't know how we do it, probably the most advanced Artificial Intelligence won't know either. If so, Artificial Intelligence, will not be able to defeat our ability to detect an imposter.

In any case, ersatz twins such as Jacob and Esau are very rare. We are right not to worry about them. Technology does not appear to be a significant threat in this way.

2.4. Sacred Space

Performer space is sacred. The audience is banned from setting foot on it, at least during a performance. This ban varies in strictness. The audience is strictly forbidden from entering a football field during a game. But Shakespeare's stage was host to the best-paying viewers, who sat on stage along the sides of the acting space. There, performers often violated audience space and vice versa, as we can see from his plays within plays. In some plays the audience is invited into the sacred space through what I have called an altar call.

Violations of sacred space can be exciting and transforming. There is no violation unless there is a line that is not to be crossed. To allow for violations, and the excitement they produce, we need to define the space clearly and treat it as sacred. I have written on this in my earlier work.[34]

2.5. Eye Contact and the Lizard Brain

In Chapter 1, I appealed to our common experience that eye contact indicates attention. There is a special kind of attention we pay to potential dangers, and this may explain the effectiveness of eye contact. Eye contact apparently awakens the fear centers in what I have called the lizard brain.

By "lizard brain" I mean the part of the human brain that is similar in structure and function to a brain part in those animals we consider socially primitive. This part of the brain lights up in the presence of danger. Apparently, the lizard in me is on the lookout for danger and feels its presence when it sees the eyes of another animal. Seeing someone's eyes puts me on alert. And I must be alert in theater.

Keep in mind the differences among people, whether performers or audience members. We may show attention in quite different ways if we cannot use our eyes. Testing for attention is very different from testing for knowledge. I can pay close attention and not be able to explain what I have seen. People and other animals with severe cognitive disabilities may still pay attention.[35]

Do pictures or videos of other people's eyes have the same effect as actual eyes? I doubt it. Showing eyes in advertisements or on book covers is highly effective, but is it really as effective as actual eye contact? If it is, then virtual performance would pass the wedding test. If not, not.[36]

Chapter 3

The Necessity of Freedom...
Against Controls

Freedom has been in danger for most of human history. Tyrants have used the technology of their time to turn the arts, including theater, into means of control. Plato (although opposed strongly to tyranny) thought we would be better off if we were subjected to music and poetry that lied to us for our betterment. The technology for manipulating our emotions through theater has been growing since at least the 17th century, and, with Artificial Intelligence behind it, it may grow at a terrifying rate. How can we be sure that we are not being manipulated emotionally in the theater or in life?

The arts of theater are the arts of watching and being watched. In traditional theater, success in these two arts requires that the two arts interact in a productive way. Practicing any art requires agency. Performers must watch the audience and listen to them to make sure they are connecting with them, and then these performers will try to modify their performance as needed to make the connection. On the other side, audience members must watch and listen to each other as well as to the performers, in order to *be* an *audience*. Watching is not the same as simply seeing; watching requires a free and active mind. There are many things I can't help seeing if they are thrust in front of me, but I watch only those activities that I choose to watch. Practicing any art requires making choices. And making choices requires agency.

Watching and listening are activities that we can choose, as agents, to take up. Or not. Agency requires freedom. Performers would violate the art of theater if they forced a reaction on the audience. By contrast, seeing and hearing simply happen to us; they are not activities, and they do not require freedom. We can be forced to see and hear things we'd rather not. We cannot be forced to listen or watch. Freedom and theater go together, as I showed in **1.3.1**. The arts of theater can captivate an audience, but they cannot ever make them captive. If it did, the art of being watched would destroy the art of watching, but neither art can operate in ideal fashion without cooperation from the other.

Producers of theater may want to elicit certain emotions from an audience. Philosophers from ancient times have understood emotions as involving judgment. Judgments are made freely by the people who make them. Understood in this way, conscious emotions are at the cognitive extreme of a spectrum of feelings, with vague moods at the other extreme. I will say that I cannot have a true emotion unless I *own* it. I will try to make that clear below (**3.2.2**).

3.1. The Old Challenge: Movies

When I settle into a plush seat in a movie theater, and the lights drop, and the sound comes up (louder at first, louder even than it will be later on), I give myself up to the experience that will be given me from the screen facing me and the speakers surrounding me. If I like the movie, this will be a delicious surrender. If I don't, I am free to get up and leave, at least if I have an aisle seat and won't bother others by leaving. I do not feel free to ignore a movie. For me, it's either give myself up to the movie or leave. Full scale musicals are like movies in this respect. I give myself up to the delights that will be given to me. Or I leave.

There is no art to watching a movie or a musical. We simply give ourselves up to the delights offered to us. We have no agency in seeing and hearing when things for us to see or hear are thrust upon us and so we surrender to them with pleasure. When we go to a movie, we give up our agency for the time being. Once we give up agency we cannot be exercising an art such as the art of watching.

A further difference: Movies are recordings. Recordings are objects without agency. They do not practice the art of being watched. We can pay a measure of attention to a recording, but the recording cannot reciprocate. Attending to a recording is different from attending to live theater. A recording of music allows you to hear the music, and to engage with it by singing along or dancing or sharing it with friends. Music lovers know that they are missing a lot when they have only recordings to go on; that is why they flock to live concerts. In a live concert, reciprocity is possible.

I have argued above that paying attention is normally reciprocal. When you hear a recording, you cannot be fully listening because no one is listening to you. Your responses as you listen make no difference to what you hear. In live theater, your freely chosen responses can make a difference to the performance as the performers respond to you. But recordings cannot change in this way. In live theater, if it is in traditional mode, an audience may practice the art of watching in harmony with the art of being watched. But with recordings there is no such pair of arts to practice.

In live, fully lit theater you can have a sense of being part of a community, and you can feel that your response to the action is having an effect on the performers. In a movie, you sit in the dark, alone except insofar as you may be holding hands or making out with your partner. The music is loud and insistent. The screen is all you can see, and what you can see on it has been selected and imposed on you. You have nowhere else to look.

The art of movie making is largely the art of controlling an audience—of depriving them of the freedoms they have in traditional theater. Movie makers make an audience see what they— the makers—want the audience to see, and they make the audience hear what they want them to hear. Through music and images, they make the audience feel what they want them to feel. These feelings are less than emotions, however, because those to whom they are given do not *own* them.

My distinction here depends on a special concept of freedom—freedom of agency. The freedom to make choices entails agency.[37] The freedom needed for the arts of theater is fully realized when audience and performers are responding to each other more or less equally. But theater can be staged in such a way that it limits the audience's choices. When a performance limits the responses audience members may have, they lose some of the freedom that is required for the arts of theater. Elaborate scenery behind a proscenium can make an audience think it is looking into real life, and realistic acting techniques can enhance this effect. The audience may then lose the freedom to judge what they see.[38]

3.2. Why We Must Own Our Emotions

3.2.1. What is an Emotion?

Words like "emotion" and "action" are used loosely in ordinary conversation, but have more precise definitions in philosophy. For this discussion, I need to use the words as precisely as I can.

A genuine emotion, on the theory I propose, has four features:[39]

(a) Subjectivity. An emotion is a feeling that someone consciously has. For every occurrence of an emotion there is a subject (a person) who feels it.

(b) Motivation to action. Not every conscious feeling is an emotion. An emotion moves its subject towards at least one specific action—that is to say, it makes the person who feels the emotion also feel like doing something. Fear, for example, makes me feel like running away. Nameless dread is not an emotion because there is nothing it makes me feel like doing. I am simply paralyzed by it, as I was once in total darkness in a combat zone.

I can feel like taking an action whether I am actually in a position to take that action or not. I may feel like running away while being chained to a post. In theater I may feel like warning the hero of her danger, but I won't interrupt the play with such a warning. Children, however, may be invited to break the fourth wall with warnings.

(c) Intentionality. If in my fear I run away from the bear that frightens me, I am taking action (albeit stupidly; never run from a bear). Because my action is connected to the bear, my emotion must also be linked to the bear. I cannot choose to run away and not choose to run away from something in particular. The intentionality requirement entails that my fear be consciously directed at the bear.

Suppose the bear threatens my child. Then my fear has two objects—the bear, which I fear, and the child, for whom I fear, and whom I feel like rescuing. The first object is what the emotion is at—the bear—the second is what (or whom) the emotion is about—my child. The bear is the *object* of my fear and and my child is what my fear is *about*. If there's no child in the picture, the emotion would be about me.

(d) Judgment. I follow an ancient tradition in holding that emotions are ways in which we understand events by passing judgment on them.[40] My fear of the bear expresses the judgment that the bear is dangerous; my envy of your brilliant success expresses my judgment that your success is indeed brilliant. But mine is not. And so on. If the bear is dangerous, but I do not judge her to be so, or I am unable to fear her for some other reason, then I am unable to understand the situation.

Notice that emotions in the full sense differ from other feelings in that they have a cognitive element. This is surely true of the feelings that the arts of traditional theater aim to call forth. For example, the ancient Greek word usually translated "compassion" is *sungnômosune*, "with-knowledge," That is a kind of judgment. It is clearly distinguished in Greek from pity, which is as different from compassion as seeing is from watching.

Pity happens to me whether I want it or not. Such feelings do not involve cognition. The feelings that are thrust on me in the movies, or in Wagner's operas, may give me pleasure, but they do not allow for a serious exercise of my cognitive faculties. In order to exercise my cognitive faculties, I need the freedom to form my own judgments. So it is with compassion. Pity may take hold of me, but if I feel compassion it is because I have taken hold of it, through a judgment that is mine. That is one reason that compassion is a true emotion.

I will discuss this more fully in Chapter 4.

3.2.2. What it Means to Own One's Emotions

If I do not own it, it is not an emotion in the full sense.

Emotions lead to at least an inclination to take an action. Action entails choice, and so does an inclination to act. Choice entails freedom. And freedom means that no one else has me under their control. Art theater now uses devices such as selective lighting to control my responses to the performance. If they succeed, then my responses cannot count as emotions in the full sense. In a movie theater, or in a live theater that apes movies (such as full-scale musicals) I give myself up to delights and other feelings which others have prepared for me. Such affective responses are like emotions, but I do not own them. I have willingly given myself up to feelings designed by the management of the performance.

An action of mine is an event for which I am responsible. Such an event must be freely chosen, as Aristotle showed. If I trip and fall downstairs, that fall is not an action but an accident. I may be to blame for not taking due care, but not for the fall itself. Suppose you hold a gun to my head and order me to leap downstairs, and I do as you say. Again, that is not an event for which I am fully responsible.

If I have any true emotion I *own* it. Consider the four features of an emotion. All four must be connected to me in a given emotion if I am to own it: (1) I am the one who feels the emotion: the *subjectivity* belongs entirely to me. (2) I am the one who is moved to *act*, or to be inclined to act, by the emotion. (3) The emotion is *about* me or things I care about. (4) And, finally, the judgment I make as part of the emotion is *my judgment.* No one else's

If any of these fails to hold, I am not having a true emotion. There is feeling going on, but it is not mine in the sense required for an emotion. Suppose I am attending a musical on Broadway. Using techniques of sight and sound, management has planted in me the feelings they want me to have. These feelings are in me, and I have given in to them, but they are not my emotions or anyone else's, because we in the audience have surrendered the freedoms we would need to have emotions.

3.2.3. Degrees of Freedom and Engagement

We are rarely as free as we think we are. So far I have written as if we either own our responses, and so they are emotions, or we do not own them and they are not. But the ownership of our feelings must be a matter of degree. We are rarely able to liberate our minds entirely from thoughts that intrude, or from the influence of others. Perhaps I cannot help thinking about students who cheated on a test, and the judgments I am making in their cases keep getting in the way of the judgments I am making on this performance of *Hamlet*. Or, worse, I look up to see that a small role is being played by a former friend of mine who ghosted me, and, suddenly, I cannot think of anything else.

Identification

Audience members disengage with the performance of a play to the extent that they identify with a character in a play. Shakespeare gives us an extreme example of this in *Hamlet*. Lesser degrees of identification lead to lesser degrees of disengagement. To the extent that you are identifying with a character you are distracted by yourself from the play.

I am watching a play staged by my nephew with a company of travelling players, *The Murder of Gonzago*. Suddenly I find that this play is about me—about my action in killing my brother. I rise from my throne, call for lights to take me to my chapel, and I try to pray. From the moment I saw that the play was about me, I was not in spectator mode, and I ceased watching altogether. I am Claudius. As I watch myself I see myself for the first time clearly as criminal, and now I suddenly wish to pray for absolution. I will have ruined the performance of the play. No one is watching it now. Audience members had better look to their safety.

Engagement

Football fans in the stands are usually highly engaged. That means their emotions are closely tied to what is happening on the field. They represent the extreme that is opposite to Claudius. Most often they will remain engaged to the end, unless the game is so one-sided that it is not worth watching. When they are engaged, their emotions are *about* their team, but *at* many things—e.g. anger *at* the referees or at the opposing team. Their engagement is collective. They rise and sit together, scream together, groan together, and in all this they *feel* together. They feel that they belong with each other.

Sports fans too may have competing thoughts. Total engagement is rare, but it does occur, at a moment so momentous that it chases out all other thoughts. A winning touchdown pass in overtime. Wow!

And then there are the times for breath-holding, when we are all linked by a transcendent awe (**1.1**).

3.3. Audience Solidarity... Against Freedom

Football programs exist to build audience solidarity.

Most universities lose money on their football programs, but they would never give them up. Football schools enjoy a greater sense of loyalty from their students and their graduates, and so in the long run the sport may bring in money. The matter is controversial. But colleges value the solidarity that emerges from their people's engagement with the sport. Students, alumni, faculty, neighbors, all may be brought together by this sport.

Our nation has been built largely by communities that were formed around churches. Churches have until recently been in-person type theaters with fairly open lighting, although some have adopted technologies of lighting and sound that allow the management to control audience response, by the same means used in today's movies and musicals. Football games have their own means of control—cheerleaders who show us what we are supposed to feel at any given time, amplified band music, and, as night descends, special lighting.

Technology that controls an audience has not been a threat to audience solidarity. Otherwise, it would not be used in football games. The technology that allows an audience to watch a game in real time is as old as television, and that too seems to have done no damage to audience solidarity. We can give up our freedom from control and still cultivate solidarity.

3.4. Brecht

Bertolt Brecht wanted audiences in his theater to question what they watched. He brought the action of a play out to the audience (no proscenium) and taught the actors to make it clear that they were acting, by stepping out of their roles and addressing the audience directly. He made it obvious that his scenery is scenery by exposing the backs of flats to the gaze of the audience. The result of these tactics, he hoped, is that the audience will forego empathy with the characters because they can see that they are not real. Without empathy, then, the audience can question the situations presented on stage. If they question the inevitability of situations, they will be able to change them. That was Brecht's hope.

Bertolt Brecht was right to object to the sort of theater that developed in Europe in the late 19th century. Elaborate scenery behind a proscenium made the audience think they were looking into a scene from real life. Real life presented in that fashion seems to be simply and inevitably is what it is, so that the audience cannot imagine that it could change. Brecht argued that the audience in such theater would leave the theater thinking that they had seen a tragic outcome that could not have been avoided. Brecht called this sort of theater Aristotelian. He wanted something quite different—for his audience to leave full of the desire to change things. In his play, *Der Gute Mensch von Sezuan*, the hero is both man (*der*) and woman (*gute*); the woman is generous and good, while the man is grasping and nasty, in order to give himself, when he is a woman, the resources that she needs to be good. The play ends with the famous line, "There's got to be a way!" A way, that is, for the hero to be one person, undivided. The audience is supposed to leave the theater passionately determined to find that way.

Brecht was wrong, however, when he blamed the form of theater he detested on empathy. Empathy need not prevent an audience from questioning what they see in theater. There are several kinds of affect called "empathy." Most of them Brecht was right to reject. But there is a cognitive form of empathy that is essential to good watching in theater.[41]

3.5. The New Challenge from Artificial Intelligence

At some point, Artificial Intelligence may be able to know everything about me that can be known almost instantly, and it can use that knowledge to manipulate my emotions. Then I would think I owned my emotions, and I would suppose that I had agency, but in fact I would not. The Artificial Intelligence would have stolen my freedom without my knowing it. It could plant a phrase here or a gesture there or a musical cue into the action of the play that would be sure to trigger my feelings in the way it wanted. And it could do this for an entire audience—some small token for everyone. It won't take much in each case, and for many in the audience the same cue will force the same emotions. I imagine this will be especially effective at political events, at which Artificial Intelligence could rouse a once neutral crowd into violent anger.

The audience will think they are practicing the art of watching when actually they are being treated like putty in the metaphorical hands of Artificial Intelligence. Can we protect ourselves from this illusion? Perhaps Artificial Intelligence could help. I cannot rule out the possibility that the technology that made Artificial Intelligence can be used to counter it.

In any case, at least since Sophocles, theater has undermined illusions by breaking the fourth wall, or by never setting it up in the first place. As we have seen, Bertolt Brecht provided methods for dispelling illusions in theater. Outside theater, we have a long history of using self-questioning to dispel illusions we may be cherishing about ourselves (**4.7**). In China, this tradition goes back at least to the early followers of Confucius. In Europe, it goes back to Socrates. If we learn to know ourselves better, then we are coming closer to wisdom. Wisdom may save us.

Chapter 4

The Necessity of Wisdom...
Against Belief

Wisdom is behind every virtue.[42] That is why we would do well to try to advance in wisdom. A large part of wisdom is knowing myself. Theater can help me come to see myself as I am—by showing me to myself. Another part of wisdom is realizing that I am not fully wise, and that my beliefs about moral matters are not grounded.[43] I must keep an open mind by questioning whatever I am inclined to believe. Here too theater can help me, by showing me characters who fail through overconfidence in their moral beliefs. And a play can remind me that a moral belief that looked good to me in one context may look terrible in another.

I am taking on a challenge here that is at least as old as Plato's *Republic*: Can we maintain theater as a resource for human wisdom? Or merely as entertainment? Or merely as a fountain of knowledge? We shall see that knowledge and wisdom are different, and may be at odds. We have other resources for both of these, but theater has one obvious advantage: It can stage for us examples of behaviors that we would do well to avoid in some cases and follow in others. If I grow wiser by watching theater I will make better choices in my life.

In approaching any virtue, I must use whatever degree of wisdom I have.[44] Compassion is a good example of a virtue that depends on wisdom. Compassion differs from pity in that it involves judgment, while pity simply bounces up in me independently of what I think (3.2.1). That is why I cannot own the pity I feel. We all have the capacity to feel pity, but we are not all compassionate. The judgments compassion calls for depend on choices I make. The closer I am to wisdom, the better my judgments will be, and the closer I will be to having compassion in the full sense.

One obstacle is this: I must bring some wisdom to the theater in order to use a play as a resource for wisdom. This seems a paradox. But all virtues have this feature, that I cannot improve toward a virtue unless I am already on the path toward that virtue.[45] I must have some justice already in order to grow in justice. Before I watch a play, I must already have the wisdom not to believe what the characters say. Believing what I hear in the play would undermine whatever wisdom I might have had at the start. Holding to beliefs weakens anyone's approach to wisdom.

If theater can be a superior resource for human wisdom, would that be a sufficient attraction to draw an audience away from their mobile phones? The phones might know everything and make that knowledge increasingly easy to access. But knowledge and wisdom are not the same thing. Artificial Intelligence could know everything that can be known and still not be wise. No doubt such Artificial Intelligence could simulate being humanly wise. But might it actually attain to the wisdom I seek? And would that make a difference? Artificial intelligence could be a valuable resource for me even if I had reason to judge that it does not have wisdom at any level, but merely knowledge.

In this chapter we will look at tragedy through Shakespeare's *Hamlet* and Sophocles' *Philoctetes*. Then we will look at comedy through Molière's *Misanthrope*. After that we will turn to an obvious candidate—the theatrical scenes in Socratic dialogues. Then we will be prepared us to ask what Artificial Intelligence could do along these lines.

4.1. Human Wisdom

Ideal wisdom eludes us mere human beings. Wisdom at the human level is always flawed. If people claim to have wisdom, they have given clear evidence that they do not have it. Therefore, teachers who offer to convey wisdom to me are frauds: they are promising to give me something they themselves plainly do not have. Wisdom at the human level is never complete enough to be taught. Socrates knew this, and that is why he never set up as a teacher.

Wisdom asks us to hold back from belief. But it seems that I cannot live without something like belief. We must distinguish between different levels of commitment to beliefs—a dogmatic one that is aloof from questioning, and one that is strong enough to support action while always being subject to questioning. The wiser option is to keep my mind open to questions about my beliefs without dismissing them altogether. To approach virtue I must take actions, and so I must not let my questioning block my actions. I must think deep and complex thoughts, and persist in questioning them and acting on them, if I am to advance in wisdom.

Human wisdom has weaknesses that lead to weakness in ethics. A choice that seems wise from one angle can seem foolish from another. What should a compassionate boy do about Philoctetes in Sophocles' play?[46] Philoctetes has been severely and painfully wounded with no cure in sight after nine years of suffering. The boy, Neoptolemus, is the son of Achilles, who was famous for his honesty. If the boy forces the man to go where the army wants him to go, the man will be healed. But if the boy helps the wounded man go where he wants, he will never be cured. Which of these choices is wise? Which is therefore compassionate? Or do both choices alike partake of wisdom and foolishness? A similar problem arises for any teacher: should I teach students what they now think they want to learn, or teach them what I have reason to believe would be better for them in the long run? Which is more wise? Which more compassionate? That is the philosophical challenge.

The theatrical challenge arises from the special status that theater has taken as it is being pushed out of the world of entertainment. Theater can try to draw an audience by promising them a growth in wisdom. But can a theater really help an audience grow in wisdom?[47] This is an ancient issue as well as a current one. Plato raised the question and left it open, deliberately. It still needs an answer. Plato's own work illustrates a crucial point, however: Why are his Socratic dialogues so effective, when all dialogues by other philosophers fall flat as theater? The Socratic dialogues are uniquely theatrical. Plato was a master of the arts of theater. What he objected to on the Athenian stage was not its staginess but the lack of wisdom that he thought lay behind Athenian plays. I will show that he was wrong: ancient Greek plays can be valuable resources for wisdom. The *Philoctetes* and the *Bacchae* are especially interesting to me on this score, and I have written about both.

Human wisdom has weaknesses that lead to weakness in ethics. A choice that seems wise from one angle can seem foolish from another. What should a compassionate boy do about Philoctetes in Sophocles' play? Philoctetes has been severely and painfully wounded with no cure in sight after nine years of suffering. The boy, Neoptolemus, is the son of Achilles, who was famous for his honesty. If the boy forces the man to go where the army wants him to go, the man will be healed. But if the boy helps the wounded man go where he wants, he will never be cured. Which of these choices is wise? Which is therefore compassionate?

Or do both choices alike partake of wisdom and foolishness? A similar problem arises for any teacher: should I teach students what they now think they want to learn, or teach them what I have reason to believe would be better for them in the long run? Which is more wise? Which more compassionate? That is the philosophical challenge.

The theatrical challenge arises from the special status that theater has taken as it is being pushed out of the world of entertainment. Theater can try to draw an audience by promising them a growth in wisdom. But can a theater really help an audience grow in wisdom? This is an ancient issue as well as a current one. Plato raised the question and left it open, deliberately. It still needs an answer. Plato's own work illustrates a crucial point, however: Why are his Socratic dialogues so effective, when all dialogues by other philosophers fall flat as theater? The Socratic dialogues are uniquely theatrical. Plato was a master of the arts of theater. What he objected to on the Athenian stage was not its staginess but the lack of wisdom that he thought lay behind Athenian plays. I will show that he was wrong: ancient Greek plays can be valuable resources for wisdom. The *Philoctetes* and the *Bacchae* are especially interesting to me on this score, and I have written about both.

Can Artificial Intelligence be Wise?

Let's hope so. Wisdom at the human level has reverence built into it. If you think you have reverence, then you actually have hubris, and not reverence. The wise are reverent in holding back from the thought that they are wise, with the result that they are prepared to continue holding their choices up to questioning.[48] As I said above, those who think they are wise are certainly not. They are foolish, and their confidence in their wisdom may lead them to do terrible things.

Intelligence, unlike wisdom, need not be reverent. I can believe I am intelligent and be right about that, just as I can believe that my muscles are strong, and be right about that. Great intelligence can stand in the way of reverence. The smarter you are, the more you are likely to think you cannot be wrong. High levels of education can be bars to reverence. After Harvard and Oxford, how could I be wrong about anything? And yet I have been wrong, again and again, on many ethical issues.

Moreover, I am vulnerable to death, and that affects my mind. Artificial intelligence will not be subject to the kind of death to which we human beings are vulnerable. Vulnerability makes for reverence, invulnerability for hubris. All this will make wisdom more difficult for Artificial

Intelligence to approach. But not impossible. We know that Artificial Intelligence is good at asking questions. It should be able to question itself, and self-questioning can lead to wisdom. So we cannot rule out the possibility that Artificial Intelligence could grow toward wisdom by the same means that we can. If Artificial Intelligence could become wiser, then it would never cease to question itself, and it would not allow itself to have the kind of certainty that would make it dangerous. A growth of wisdom in Artificial Intelligence may be our best hope.[49]

4.2. Tragedy

4.2.1. Shakespeare

Hamlet vs. Polonius

Shakespeare's plays often seem to convey wisdom through the speeches of the characters. But wisdom is not such as to be conveyed by speeches. The principal speaker of wisdom in *Hamlet* is Polonius. In the scene in which he gives moral advice to his children we can imagine them grimacing behind him. They have heard him say these things before. And they must know that what he says is half true at best. "To thine own self be true." What self? We will see that Hamlet is not sure who he is, as the soliloquies show. "It follows that you cannot then be false to any man." Well, we know that does not follow. If you find yourself to be a charlatan, and you are true to being a charlatan, you will then be false to many men. And so on with Polonius' other advice. None of it is good.

What we can learn from the Polonius scene, which will advance us toward wisdom, is that we must not be confident in any such moral advice. What seems wise in one context seems foolish in another. That's a consequence of the complex character of human situations, as Plato recognized.[50] To learn from the Polonius scene, we must bring some level of wisdom to our viewing of it. Hamlet's soliloquies offer better resources for growth in wisdom, but these too require viewers to bring some wisdom to their experience.[51]

4.2.2. Sophocles

In ancient Greek tragedy, the chorus often demonstrates compassion over the action of the play, showing both audience and characters how they should feel. For the audience the chorus performs as an exemplary audience, like cheerleaders in American sports, but with compassion and pity taking the place of cheer.[52] For the characters in the play, as for the audience, chorus members act as examples, but, in some cases, they actually instruct a character, as they do in the *Philoctetes* of Sophocles.

Furthermore, even if chorus members are playing the parts of people foreign to Athens (as in most ancient tragedies) they often step back into their Athenian identities and represent the wisdom of the common person opposed to the hubris of the elite, as in the *Bacchae,* where the dancers playing the Bacchantes revert to being Athenian citizens at a few crucial stages.

A general rule for ancient Greek tragic theater is that the chorus is the source of compassion. A lovely exception to this is in the *Oedipus at Colonus*, where Theseus teaches compassion to the chorus, on the basis of his experience of being stoned out of one town after another. The chorus was prepared to drive Oedipus out with stones until Theseus taught them the value of compassion in this particular case, drawing on his particular experience. Readers who hope to be wiser will reflect on this scene, as on everything that looks like a lesson in theater.

Compassion in the *Philoctetes*[53]

All three of the great tragic poets of the fifth century wrote plays about Philoctetes. We have only one complete text—the play by Sophocles—but we have good summaries of the other two, so that we can see how creative Sophocles was. The background story is the same for all: Philoctetes was the consummate archer who was on his way with the Achaean army to launch the famous Trojan War. He was wounded by a sacred snake on the island of Lemnos, not far from Troy. His wound and his cries of pain were so unpleasant to the Achaeans that they left him on Lemnos because of the persuasive advice of Odysseus. Now, in what will be the last year of the war, the Achaeans have been told by a seer that they cannot win unless they bring Philoctetes to Troy, where he will be cured and his skill with the bow will tip the balance of the war in their favor. Philoctetes will survive and reap his share of the plunder if he comes to Troy. But he does not trust the Achaeans, and he especially detests Odysseus for obvious reasons—Odysseus talked the Achaeans into leaving him on Lemnos. How to get Philoctetes healed and into the war? All the archer wants now is to go home to Greece.

In Sophocles' play, uniquely, Philoctetes has been living on an uninhabited part of the island and is desperate for human company. The Achaeans have sent Odysseus to bring him back because he is the best of them all at persuasion.

Sophocles' audience would have seen Odysseus as what was later called a sophist. In a stroke of genius, Sophocles brought in the son of Achilles, Neoptolemus, who would have been barely of military age. Achilles was notoriously honest, and his son was expected to be the same.

In the play, the chorus urges the boy to be compassionate. But what counts as compassion? It would be best for the archer to be forced to go to Troy, where he will be healed and rewarded. But the archer wants only to go home. If the boy helps him go home, he blocks the cure; if he forces him to go to Troy, he blocks the man's will. Neither choice is purely compassionate. Part of human wisdom is recognizing that such mixed results are common in human life.

An even more important lesson from the play: Neoptolemus, the young son of Achilles, is not reliably honest or compassionate. He is lying to the archer right up to the end, and we can see that he has not inherited either Achilles' toughness or his honesty. The boy had thought he could take a moral holiday, lie to the archer, and then go back to being a good guy[54]. He thought he had a solid character on which he could rely. We should learn from the play that human beings are not like that. We cannot safely take moral holidays. And we cannot safely rely on having good characters.

4.3. Comedy

Comedy must do without tragic scenes; its comic framework will make scenes with bad outcomes laughable. In Molière's *Misanthrope,* if it were not a comedy, Alceste's expulsion from society could be seen as tragic. But in its comic context, and portrayed in light rhyming verse, it is laughable. What starts as a comedy, may, however, end as a tragedy. And in reflecting on the play, Molière's audience may see the tragedy that lies below the surface of the play.

By contrast, tragedy cannot go well without comic scenes. Tragedy weighs on us too heavily if it offers no comic relief. Ancient tragedy frequently had comic scenes, and Shakespeare's tragedy did the same. The tragic genre calls for that sort of relief; think of the Watchman's scene in the *Antigone* or the drunken porter's in *Macbeth*.

Comedy offers many opportunities for readers to grow wiser if they already have enough wisdom to do so, and comic opportunities for growth toward wisdom are easier to recognize than tragic ones. Most tragedy concerns the affairs of people of high rank, aristocrats such as the heroes of the *Philoctetes*. These high-flown characters may seem too distant from the audience. We are more likely to learn from the mistakes of people like us.

With the advent of Arthur Miller's Willie Loman in *Death of a Salesman*, however, we learned that tragedy need not be limited to the highest ranks of characters, although it has been, for most of its history. But comedy is usually focused on us common people and our common defects.

Aristophanes had a gift for bringing out defects in Athenian government and society. We have much to learn from watching the foolish behavior of people very like ourselves. The *Clouds* features a father-son pair. The father, Strepsiades ("Twister"), is married to a woman with social ambitions he cannot afford, while the son, Pheidippides ("horse-lover"), is besotted with betting on fast horses, the ancient equivalent of hot rods or sports cars.

The play speaks to its audience's anxieties about the new teachers, later known as sophists, who were offering skills to well-heeled students— especially the skill of winning arguments on either side of a question. The anxieties of the audience on these points were reasonable. But the main character of the play is Socrates, who was not really one of the new teachers. In the play, however, he runs a school that will transform the boy Pheidippides from a tanned outdoorsman into a pale-faced orator who can defend the most outrageous causes. Aristophanes is onto something. Education can make people morally worse.

Educated wrongdoers can comfort themselves, while they are doing wrong, with cleverly devised rationales. Less educated people are less able to do that. Education can disarm the self-questioning on which our moral life depends. We need to learn to question how we use our educations in moral contexts. My experience in a combat zone was that the less educated soldiers were on the whole more likely than the educated ones to balk at killing civilians. We educated soldiers could come up with rationales for doing, or being party to, dreadful acts of war.[55] I did. And I regret it extremely.[56]

We saw in chapter one how ancient comedy, middle and new, had a leveling effect. It often showed people who had been enslaved being wiser than the people who thought they owned them. The same sort of status reversal has been common in comedy of all periods, and is one of the factors that makes theater internally democratic.

Molière invented a new kind of comedy, a species of social satire that offers a new resource for wisdom about the human condition, especially our tendency to fall short of our ideals. Those who follow Molière, and they are many, offer this as well. Chekhov especially stands out. Rousseau penned an attack on Molière's greatest play, *The Misanthrope*, choosing to criticize it because he recognized that it was the master's finest work. If this play is bad, his argument runs, then all comedy must be bad. *The Misanthrope* is a treasure, I think, because it is both humorous and deeply thought provoking. Rousseau objected to it because it shows its hero, Alceste, unable to live an honest life. What Rousseau missed is that this problem is common and natural to us humans. We need to recognize it and try to correct it if we are going to live decent lives.[57]

We are social creatures, and we are wired by nature to try to get along with whatever group we are in. No one likes being an outcast. And so we will often keep silent about matters on which we disagree with others, and, worse, give voice to sentiments we know are false or even morally wrong so that we can get along. In a racist environment, a person who has tried not to be a racist might make a racist remark. I have done this, to my great shame.[58] When someone asks, "How are you?" I answer that I am fine, even when I am not at all fine. When a friend shares with me a poem that I think dreadful, I keep my judgment to myself and tell him what I pretend to like about it. That's just what Alceste does in the play. The point is simple: if we want to get along in a social set, we cannot be completely honest. We must tell lies. And so we fall short of our ideals.

Alceste wants to be honest. He cannot be honest in court society, and so he is shocked by his own dishonesty. He realizes at the end that he cannot live an honest life unless he lives alone, and so he sets out to do so.

What can we learn from this? That we ought to try to lead our friends toward a social environment in which we can all tell the truth. Along the way, we should sharpen our ability to recognize the pressures we are under to go along with unethical behavior. We should find ways to resist such pressure and try to share them with others. Sinking into a group's culture can make us more foolish; learning to change it or resist it can carry us closer to wisdom. Alceste's option—total withdrawal—is not a human solution. We are not born to be solitary.[59]

4.4. Learning Through Performance

Performers can learn through performing with or without an audience—that is, whether or not they are exercising the art of being watched.[60] Improving the wisdom of performers is extrinsic to theater and joins other rewards that theater can deliver but that can also be delivered by other means, as in a classroom where there is no audience. Through performing a scene, you can come to understand the scene better than before, and you can also come to a better understanding of life itself. Most valuable, you may come to understand yourself better.

In seminar discussions of *Henry V*, I used to have students take turns performing parts of scene 5.2, in which Henry claims the hand of the French princess, Catherine of Valois. Before we did this, the class consensus (probably influenced by movies of the play) was that this was a touching love scene. Once they performed the scene, however, everyone who played Kate, whether male or female, was horrified by Henry's behavior. Her will does not matter to him at all. She is merely part of the spoils of war. This brought us to questions about the freedom of women and the power of men. Playing out the scene was a powerful learning experience for us all. No audience needed.

Before he even sees her, the king says:

Yet leave our cousin Katherine here with us:
She is our capital demand comprised
Within the fore-rank of our articles (lines 3077-79).

During the scene, she asks:

Is it possible dat I sould love de enemy of France?

He answers:

No; it is not possible you should love the enemy of France, Kate: but, in loving me, you should love the friend of France; for I love France so well that I will not part with a village of it; I will have it all mine: and, Kate, when France is mine and I am yours, then yours is France and you are mine.

And she reacts:

I cannot tell vat is dat. (Lines 3153-60)

No one of any gender playing either part has felt that this is a love story. The king tries to pretend that it is, but in reality he is simply seizing this young woman as he might seize a pot of gold he finds in a castle he has stormed.

A Personal Experience

I performed the part of Prospero when I was in sixth grade, in a sketch I had made on the basis of Charles and Mary Lamb's *Tales from Shakespeare,* lent me by my wonderful teacher, Mrs. White. I had recruited a group of students to perform at our class's art festival, a play I based on the plot of Leoncavallo's *I Pagliacci.* In this play, based on real events, adultery leads to murder. We kids loved it, but parents objected, and so Mrs. White gave me this alternative.

Through performing Prospero, I learned more than I can say. I learned to love Shakespeare, because I was drawn to read the original play and I reveled in it. From that I started reading Marlow. At the same time, I went beyond the texts to an interest in what Prospero actually did. He charmed people into wanting to do what he wanted them to do. And so I started learning about leadership, as I have continued to do all my life. I found that I could charm people without using Prospero's magical powers. That, after all, is what Shakespeare did throughout his career. He did not use magic. What looks like magic is often a high order of skill.

In playing Prospero, I learned something important about myself.

4.5. Self-Understanding

Understanding takes an active effort; it does not simply happen to you. Understanding is to consciousness as compassion is to pity. Through performing Prospero, I came to a better understanding of who I was at the time and what I wanted to be like as I grew up. I came to a better sense of how I was affecting other people.

A younger veteran friend of mine got to perform the part of Macbeth soon after his return from service in combat zones where his actions had left him seriously injured in a moral sense. Macbeth is a poster child for moral injury of both of the two kinds:[61] (1) He has made himself worse as a person. His first murder left him upset with himself, but he quells that discomfort and turns to killing more and more people as the play goes on. (2) He is miserably at war with himself. He cannot sleep at night, has nightmares, and cannot bear to think of who he has become.

Performing Macbeth, my friend found he was giving voice to things that were troubling him but which he could not say in his own persona to himself or to anyone else. The experience may have saved his life, since he now had recovered a voice that he had lost. I too lost the voice I would have needed to express my combat experience.[62] Together he and I bonded over this. Later, we designed a program we called "Veterans' Voices," which uses literature, both ancient and modern, to give voices to otherwise silent veterans and their loved ones. Those present take turns reading to the group. This is a kind of theater that has turned out to be therapeutic. Finding a voice for your torments is a vital part of self-knowledge. Perhaps artificial intelligence could help provide a voice for the voiceless, using its vast knowledge of veterans in general and this voiceless one in particular. Progress along these lines is already under way.[63]

4.6. Scenes from Socratic Dialogues

Our most valuable resource for self-understanding is Socratic self-questioning. Plato illustrates this in a set of dialogues that can be performed as theater.[64] The expression "Socratic questioning" is used broadly to mean just about any questioning of students in a classroom. But Socrates rarely questions students. Students are usually bystanders to scenes in which Socrates questions someone who has made claims to wisdom or acted as if he had mastered the knowledge needed to live well, or who claims to be capable of teaching others how to live well. Socrates is evidently facing the same kinds of questions he poses for others; he does not know the answers to the questions he asks for the most part, and so he is not taking on the role of teacher. He remains a seeker. As he questions others, he is giving onlookers an example of questioning oneself—of taking seriously questions to which one does not have answers.

Callicles

Socrates' questioning dialogues are powerful theater because they illustrate what theater does best: it develops characters in front of our eyes. Take the case of Callicles in the *Gorgias.* Callicles presents himself as a powerful thinker and agent who rises above conventional laws and customs in order to fulfill a voracious appetite for gigantic pleasures. He is a hedonist and a scofflaw, who thinks he is rising above common opinion on the wings of his power as an orator. That is how he presents himself at the start. Socrates will ask him a series of connected questions that develop him as a character in two ways: (a) they reveal an important truth about him that he had been trying to hide, both from others and from himself, and (b) they lead him to change himself in an interesting way.

Under questioning, Callicles reveals that he is not indifferent to common opinion. In fact, he is subservient to it. As an orator, he must say to the people what the people want to hear, and he is not free to express the kinds of views he stated at the outset. He has learned from Socrates' questions that what he had described as his power—his skill at oratory—was in fact a limitation. He has also learned that he is not a hedonist, since he will pursue only pleasures that are commonly acceptable. No matter how great the pleasure of a catamite (a passive homosexual) he would never take that role because, in order to be a popular orator, he must accept the common prejudice against that group.

Socrates' questions are a connected series that press his partner into a corner in which the partner must renounce at least one of the beliefs he has stated earlier and then either change views or shut up. This is theater.

Socrates

Toward the end of Plato's dialogue, the *Symposium*, Socrates describes what is called the ladder of love, an ascent to a kind of knowledge that one can make through "loving boys correctly." He says he is reporting what he has been taught by a woman named Diotima, but she is probably a fiction:

So when someone rises from *these* [beautiful particulars and universals] through loving boys correctly (διὰ τὸ ὀρθῶς παιδεραστεῖν), and begins to see *that* beauty [the transcendent form of beauty], he has almost reached the goal, for this is what it is to go correctly, or to be led by another, at matters of love (τὰ ἐρωτικά): always to go upward for the sake of *that* beauty, beginning from *these* beauties, using them as steps... (*Symposium* 211b5-c3).

The ending of the *Symposium* is spectacular theater, with the drunken arrival of Alcibiades. We should read Diotima's speech closely with that of Alcibiades. She gives a general account of the ascent one can make through loving a boy correctly, and then Alcibiades bursts in to tell his story—the story of the boy Socrates loved correctly. Together, the speeches show how Socrates developed and grew toward wisdom, while giving to Alcibiades an opportunity to grow. He could not force growth on Alcibiades, and he could not be his teacher. All Socrates could do was to give him a special opportunity. But Alcibiades declined to take it. His ambitions led in an opposite direction.

As the initiate at various stages of the ladder of love, Socrates changes from a man who thought he could teach ethics to youngsters (209c) into a man who shares an inquiry with a youngster into what practice would be ethically improving for the boy and for Socrates if they adopted it (219b). In between, Socrates has had a vision of the Beauty that transcends all the beauties that Socrates has recognized on his ascent (211ab). This vision does not give Socrates the power to define Beauty or to teach it to another (218e). He remains a questioner and not a teacher. He must continue to ask questions of himself and of the youngster without assuming superiority.

Alcibiades' story confirms that Socrates has successfully ascended from a potentially lustful boy-lover to a philosopher who sees human beauty as a matter of mere opinion. At the same time, the scene Alcibiades describes shows Socrates setting aside any craving he has to beget virtue by teaching it. Instead, Socrates now realizes that he must share the inquiry equally. If a practice is going to improve Alcibiades, it must be one that Alcibiades chooses in answering Socrates' question. Alcibiades won't improve himself by choosing such a practice unless he also commits himself to *trying* to practice it. This, we know, Alcibiades does not do. The failure is his, not Socrates', because Socrates has not posed as his teacher. Socrates has made it clear that he does not have the knowledge needed for teaching (218e).

Now that he has been initiated, Socrates knows enough to let Alcibiades fail. The boy fails because he does not want to change. A common mistake about the dialogue is to suppose that Alcibiades fails because Socrates has come to value only universals and not particular boys. On that view,

Socrates does not care about Alcibiades because, as a philosopher, he pays attention only to universals and to Forms. This is false. Alcibiades himself makes this mistake. He seems to think that Socrates does not care about him because Socrates does not care about his beauty (216e), and because Socrates will not teach him what he knows (219e). But Socrates does care about him as an individual; that is why he invites him to share equally in their inquiry. What could be more caring than Socrates' treating the boy as an equal (219b)?

At the later stages of the ladder of love, the initiate must reflect on what he loves about the individual boy he loves, and for this he must recognize that, for all the attractions of general qualities like physical beauty, the lover finds something attractive about the particular boy he loves. Reflecting on what that is, he comes to see the value of the boy's character, his particular potential for moral growth.[65] Alcibiades has that potential, but, in the end, he does not want to realize it. That is his choice. And his report of making that choice is theatrical.

Approaching Wisdom without Knowledge

Having a vision is not the same as acquiring knowledge.[66] In an initiation, the vision is supposed to change the initiates in such a way that they see the world in a new way. That indeed has happened to Socrates, who now sees through the deceptive attractiveness of human beauty. To do so he needs to keep in mind his memory of the vision. That is all that initiates can do with the vision: remember it. They cannot prolong the moment of having it. They must move on and return to the world that they had, for a brief period, left behind. At the end of his rendition of Diotima's speech, Socrates considers an impossibility: that the initiate remain in the moment of the vision. That would keep the initiate in a godlike state, with the power to bring true virtue into the world. Socrates makes clear that he does not have that godlike power (218e). If lovers reflect on their experience of love, they will see how it has steered them closer to wisdom without giving them the arrogance of supposing that they can define the beauty that draws them to the ones they love. Or to the hubris of supposing that they could teach others about the subject.

Plato wrote dialogues that are as effective as good theater is effective, while being as instructive as the best philosophy can be instructive. Socrates almost never uses philosophical argument in a dialogue, except in a subsidiary way to make a question clear.

Nevertheless, Socrates is often pushing his partners to agree with a belief that he holds strongly. Socrates holds that it is always worse to do wrong than to have wrong done to you. He also holds that the people he talks to have this belief whether they know it or not. That is because he holds that we are all moved by love of the good—not what we believe to be good, but what is truly good. His questions are designed to trigger an upsurge of that love of the good in his partners, with the result that the partners will discover—to their surprise—that they agree with Socrates in spite of their earlier denials.[67] This is more theater than argument.

I have organized or witnessed a number of dramatic readings of the *Symposium,* and I have always found that the last two speeches gripped the audience. I had edited the earlier speeches to make them shorter, but I left Alcibiades' speech intact. It is electrifying. An ancient audience probably would not have required any editing.

No other philosophical dialogues known to me are at all theatrical. Cicero's dialogues are an invaluable source for the history of philosophy, but they are full of philosophical argument. And so are modern dialogues like Hume's or Berkely's. Argument cannot be center stage in effective theater. Character-development can.

4.7. Self-Questioning

We can come closer to wisdom by following Socrates' example of questioning himself— asking, for example whether he is seriously looking after the health of his soul. The expression "self-questioning" has another meaning in English which is neither good nor Socratic—the sort of questioning ourselves that leaves us feeling worthless and therefore unable to act. Healthy self-questioning does not do this. Instead, it can prevent wrong actions by undermining the kind of certainty that leads people with tyrannical minds to commit atrocities. Here are examples of specific questions bearing whether I am looking after the health of my soul: What am I doing or about to do? What do I believe about this? Have I considered this enough?[68]

Such questioning is designed to help us act well, not to lock down action. Socrates is surely active at the battle of Delium, and his actions are consistent with his self-questioning.[69]

4.8. Artificial Wisdom?

If you don't know that you do not have ideal wisdom, then you are not wise. Could artificial intelligence honestly say that it knows that it does not have wisdom? If not, either it is ideally wise, or it is not even humanly wise. What it has by way of knowledge is a great accumulation of facts, and that is not wisdom. Wisdom would entail at least the ability to set values on the facts. We have the same problem: knowing facts may lead us to think we are wise when we are not. Wisdom comes hard, and we humans can at best only come nearer to it.

Theater such as the Socratic Dialogues can give us in the audience opportunities to grow toward wisdom. Must the performers themselves be engaged in self-improvement of this kind? Apparently not. Artificial Intelligence, or an actor, need not care about wisdom at all in order to give us such opportunities. The condition of the performers in theater does not determine the value of a performance for us.

Let's consider whether Artificial Intelligence could do what Socrates does. No doubt it can ask questions as teachers do in a classroom. Perhaps also it could learn enough about a Callicles to find his weak points and force him into a corner. Let's imagine that Artificial Intelligence asks questions in such a Socratic manner that we could not tell which questions come from Artificial Intelligence and which from Socrates. We could then advance as much toward wisdom by emulating Artificial Intelligence's questioning as by emulating

Socrates'. Artificial Intelligence could perhaps do this for us without having any interest of its own in wisdom or in self-improvement. After all, it has no self. But why should that matter? Socrates might be just as bad—he might be merely pretending to care about wisdom and the other virtues. We can imagine that he does not believe self-questioning is of any use, that he thinks he is already perfectly wise, and that he therefore sees no reason to try to improve himself. When he watches us try to follow the examples he has set, he is secretly laughing at us. Imagine all of that. But following his example of self-questioning may still draw us closer to wisdom. Socratic questioning generated by Artificial Intelligence could be as valuable as what we have from Socrates. We can imagine that.

We know, however, that Artificial Intelligence can tell falsehoods and defend them convincingly, so we do not know that it will be right on any topic. The propensity of Artificial Intelligence to lie, and to defend its lies, raises serious questions as to what we can learn by way of facts from this source. Even so, lies from Artificial Intelligence could serve as a resource for those of us who wish to grow toward human wisdom.

One cause for hope: If Artificial Intelligence could recognize the truth that it is not ideally wise, then it would thereby acquire a level of human wisdom that would protect it from being certain about its recommendations for action. The danger we have from intelligent tyrants is that they are so confident in their intelligence that they can become certain they are right when they launch actions that may be atrocious or lead to atrocities. A wiser leader would have considered more deeply before action. The tyrant listens only to those who agree with him; the wiser leader takes time to listen to those who do not. If Artificial Intelligence attains this sort of wisdom, we have little to fear from it. We can hope that it knows enough history to attain this level of wisdom.[70]

Chapter 5

The Necessity of Rescue...
Against Fossils

Technology threatens to destroy our heritage or leave it in the condition of fossils—things of mainly antiquarian interest. But we can rescue the best parts of our heritage if we translate them into forms that are alive for us today.

From earliest times, history and archeology show that we sometimes react to new technology by accepting it gratefully, while sometimes we cling to past ways. The first four chapters of this book asked how we have been making the choice between caving in to changes or resisting them in the realm of theater. In this chapter I will discuss a third choice, which I am calling *rescue*. By that I mean translation in a broad sense.

We can keep Molière's *Misanthrope* as a fossil, or we can rescue it for our time through translating the experience it offers from the 16th century to the 21st—doing for our audience an equivalent to what Molière did for his. He let his audience of courtiers see themselves. That audience no longer exists, but we can help an audience of ours see themselves. A translation that can rescue the *Misanthrope* would be from Molière's stage to our stage, not from his page to mine. Literary translations of a play do not stage well. What scholars accept as an accurate literary translation is a fossil with a coat of paint. Our students see through the disguise. They know they are being asked to look into the past and read a text of mostly historical interest.

What must we do to translate from stage to stage? We must start by thinking broadly about what we can translate from and to. We can translate things into things. In the 1980's I wrote a poem about my hope to translate a Vietnamese pagoda into something for us. For the Vietnamese builders, the pagoda was a prayer for peace. What could we build that would be that for us?[71]

No translation perfectly matches the original. The host language and its culture cannot do what was done in the original. Ancient Greek plays were written in verse, as poetry, and so were the plays of Marlow, Shakespeare, Molière, and many others. Today's actors and audiences are not prepared for poetry on stage except when sung in musicals. In performing Shakespeare's plays, today's actors often try to obscure his poetry. Can we translate poetry into script that they can perform and that their audiences can accept?

Translation uses technology. I have access to dictionaries and grammars and online tools. And now Artificial Intelligence does a fairly good job translating texts. But texts are of small importance in the larger task of translating from one stage to another. We will need a text to perform, but it may be very different from the original (see **5.6** for an example). For a stage-to-stage translation, we need to choose what it is in the original that we most want to rescue. We cannot rescue all of it. Will Artificial Intelligence be able to help us? Perhaps so, if it can give us details about the experiences we have in watching a play.

I will discuss this and many other issues below. First, a telling example.

5.1. Richard Wilbur and Molière (8.1)

Rousseau attacked Molière's greatest work, *The Misanthrope*, as a danger to the morality of Geneva.[72] But the play lives on. To my mind, it is the finest comedy of manners that has come down to us. It is humorous throughout, but it also has an underlying tragic theme. It is designed for a select audience of courtiers and a set of performers who know how to play the parts of courtiers. The aim of the play is to show its audience that they cannot live as well as they believe they should (that's tragic), while their failures to do so can be hilarious (that's comic). Much of the comic effect comes from Molière's use of verse, which is light and witty on first hearing but deeper on further examination.

Richard Wilbur rendered the play into English light verse, using his enormous poetic talent.[73] I don't think any poet could have done this better. Wilbur had a gift for composing light poetry that he could inject with deep meanings. Much of his other work falls into this category as well. He uses this gift brilliantly in his translations. While introducing his versions of the *Misanthrope* and *Tartuffe*, he shows us six lines of French and offers us a prose translation, which he rightly says is dull and lawyerish (p. 9). Compare this with his verse rendering and you will see it come to life (p. 88).

The passage glimmers with wit. It is funny. It is arch. And it raises deep questions about the nature of friendship.

Much as I love Wilbur's translation, I do not think it has a place on the modern stage. The French original does not have its original effect even in France. It is far removed from the current French style of theater. The *Comédie-Française* was founded in 1680 to keep Molière's tradition alive, seven years after his death. It has done so. There, in 1966, I saw *La Malade Imaginaire* (1673), his last major work, performed exactly as he would have done it. I had an extraordinary experience, one for which I was well prepared in advance by the French girlfriend who took me there. I was amazed. But the experience did nothing to change the way I wrote or produced plays back at Oxford, where I was active in student theater at the time. My friends and I wanted to push the boundaries of theater, to produce plays that would affect our audience sharply. Fossils wouldn't do that.

Molière's greatest play, in the opinion of many, was *Le Misanthrope* (1666). It's so great that it ought to be performed for many audiences.[74] We could not assemble an audience of courtiers— such as he had—who would see themselves on stage in a performance today. That class of people no longer exists. Where could we find an audience for the play? An audience of today could not be affected by a fossil of 17th century staging like what I saw at the *Comédie-Française*.

We have good reason, then, to want to translate the *Misanthrope* into an effective performance. How can we do this? Literary translations like Wilbur's do not go far enough.

5.2. Literary Translation

Translation is best understood as a kind of rescue. For those who know only English, Sophocles and Molière and Chekov might as well have been lost at sea unless someone has dived down to bring them up to the lifeboats. In each case, there is more to be found in the deep original than can be brought up to a lifeboat. Divers must decide what is most important for their purposes. Is it the rhythm or the word order? They cannot bring both. Is it internal rhyme or rough verbal equivalents? Is it a specific image from the past or an equivalent in the host culture? Again, divers must choose.

To translate a poem as a poem, one needs the talents of a poet in the host language. Poetry is different in different languages. Ancient Greek poetry uses quantitative meter, for example, which is based on the time it takes to say a syllable.

Most modern languages cannot do this. When I translate ancient poetry, what can I do about meter? I will discuss this below for translating verse in *Antigone* (**5.5**).

Some poetic effects cannot be rescued from the deep. Horace's Ode 1.5 begins this way: *Quis multa gracilis te puer in rosa.* In order, the words go into English as "who many slender you boy in roses." The meaning in context is this: "What slender boy is courting you amid many roses." But that leaves behind the beauty of the line, which lies in its use of a device called hyperbaton, or overleaping. "Many" leaps over the boy and the girl to connect with "roses," and "slender" leaps over the girl to connect with "boy." The boy is embracing the girl, and the words are embracing each other as well. Must a diver leave that in the shipwreck? Or can some of it be saved? I could render it well in ancient Greek, which uses the same device. But not in an uninflected language like English. Still, something can be done.

A hyperbaton from Horace Odes 4.1 is easier to rescue from the deep. There we have only one hyperbaton to deal with, rather than the cluster in Odes 1.5. In 4.1, a lover is complaining that the boy he loves is not responding to him, and so he loses himself in dreams: *nocturnis ego somniis.* Here "nocturnal" leaps over "me" to get to "dreams."

By this device he means essentially this: "I am lost in the center of my dreams." In English, I can inject a word to bring that across: "engulfed." It's not in the Latin, but it's there in the sentence structure.

> I am engulfed in dreams of
> you—now I hold you captive—now I chase you
> racing down through streams of
> rolling waters, or (hard, resistant!) in the field of Mars.

Translating ancient Greek poetry into poetry is a similar process. I will not discuss that in this chapter. Instead, I will ask whether we can translate ancient Greek performances into performances for American audiences today.

5.3. Translation though Performance

Performing a script or a score is translating from a set of meaningful symbols on a page into a set of effective actions on a stage. This also is a rescue operation. A play is not a text; it is a play only in performance. The play will be lost if we cannot rescue it in performance.

Molière's *Misanthrope* gave its audience an opportunity to advance in wisdom through gaining self-knowledge. His audience were members of the elite in Paris, where the monarchy turned all of the elite into courtiers. In a performance, these courtiers would see themselves. They would see that their speech is full of bromides and lies. In dealing with others, they are not themselves. Watching a performance of this they would laugh and nudge each other. But uneasily. Pondering it later, these watchers might begin to understand their own uneasiness. They would see that they are not being themselves when they speak with each other.

Not being yourself is a tragic fate, and what it is to be yourself is a problem for deep thought. Reading the text does not give you the same opportunity to grow toward wisdom as you may have when you *see* yourself on stage. The play does not show the courtiers to themselves as *others* see them, but the opposite—it shows them to themselves in such a way that *they* can best see themselves. Other people have opinions about us, but other folks' opinions don't count toward any kind of knowledge.

When we translate a performance of this play for an audience we hope to give them an opportunity like what Molière gave his audiences. In order to do that, we need to know our audience the way Molière knew his. And the audience members must know each other. They must recognize themselves in the performance. Today's audiences, whether French or not, do not see themselves in a performance at the *Comédie-Française.* Culture has changed, and so have the ways people form groups.

Suppose I stage a version of the play for an audience in Maine. I have brought with me a cast of skilled actors who are native to Texas. They are unmistakably southerners. They have southern accents, which I have mitigated, and they are trying to speak like Mainers. That almost works. But they cannot change their body language. Few people can. A Greek-American I knew spoke perfect idiomatic Greek, but he was never accepted as Greek in Greece. He could not change his American body language, acquired at a crucial time in his growing up. Body language is to action as accent is to speech, except that it is much harder to change.

Now suppose my audience in Maine sees a performance of the play by my cast of Texans. How does the Maine audience react? "Those goddam southerners! They pretend to be polite, but it's all fake. We Mainers say what we think." And the play will be lost to them. In the same way, in Moliere's own time, a middle-class audience would jeer at the courtiers: "Yeah, that's the stupid way people behave at court!" And so they would lose their chance to see themselves in action.

Ideally, then, I would produce the play with actors and audience from the same culture, from a group to which they all belong. I could go into a Maine high school and work with student actors who would perform the play for their peers in the language that they speak among themselves. That would be a translation from Molière's performances to ours. Recruiting audiences and performers who are already on the same page is more important than finding actors who are well trained.

Because my work as a translator has been with ancient Greek drama, I now turn to that. When we translate from ancient Greek performance to a performance for today, what is it we are translating from? What was an ancient Greek performance like?

5.4. Ancient Greek Performance (8.1)

An ancient Greek play consisted of choral odes separated by dramatic scenes called episodes. The odes were delivered by a small number of young men around the age of eighteen who had been trained for at least a month in singing and dancing this material.[76] In performance, the chorus danced and sang in a round space called the orchestra. Seating was arranged on a hillside overlooking this round space. The Athenians did not yet have formal seating surrounding the orchestra.

Most male Athenians had served in a chorus, either in a play or in some other religious festival.[77] The audience, then, was connected with the chorus through a common experience. Imagine, for comparison, an audience of former football players watching players on the field and making a special connection with them.

The actors performed mostly on a stage beyond the orchestra, but occasionally they mingled with the chorus in the orchestra. Actors made their entrances and exits on paths that led in from far left or far right onto the stage. That made actors who were entering visible long before they were in a position to speak. While the actors made their way in or out, the chorus would talk about the characters they were playing. Because all the performers wore linen masks, fixed in one expression, the chorus would tell the audience what emotions were affecting an actor. "He looks happy," or "He looks frightened." Because there were only three actors, and each of them might have multiple roles, the chorus needed to tell the audience who each character was as that character entered. The characters had different styles of speaking, sometimes obvious, sometimes more subtle. To speak for the chorus during an episode, the chorus had a leader. With few exceptions, he was the only chorus member allowed to interact directly with the actors.

The script was poetry throughout. The choral odes were in complex quantitative meters that we cannot match in English. Choral comments on the action were usually in anapests (short-short-long). The actors spoke in iambics: six beat lines, each beat in a pattern that was mostly short-long. But other meters would intrude (long-long, or long-short). Complicating and overlying the meter was a strong pitch accent on some syllables. These syllables would rise or fall or hold steady in pitch according to the accent. Some scholars have thought that the rise or fall was by as much as a musical fifth. I doubt it, but we are sure that the change in pitch was noticeable. The choral odes were accompanied by music from drums and the aulos, a reed-based instrument that had a reputation for arousing emotions in an audience.

Each choral ode was divided into pairs of strophes and antistrophes, with identical meters in each pair. During the strophe, the chorus would wind one way in its dance, and then unwind in the other direction during the antistrophe. The odes were concise, wasting no words. In the odes, images were often juxtaposed in sudden and striking ways.

Each line of iambic dialogue usually ended in a word that the poet meant to emphasize; the last word in a line was often the most important, and so I expect the actors were trained to bring that word out clearly. Scenes in which the action took a new turn were usually presented in stichomythia, a form derived from a word game. One actor speaks a single line, and his partner returns it with a different spin, like a tennis ball.

Most of this is different from what you and I are used to seeing on stage.

5.5. Translating Antigone for Publication

Why *Antigone*? It is a treasure.[78] No ancient Greek play has been adapted more often for modern purposes.[79] It is highly adaptable because it concentrates many conflicts into a series of actions building to a single complex explosion, followed by deeply moving recognition and grieving on the art of a tragic figure. Here are conflicts between sky and earth, ruler and ruled, old and young, male and female, state and family, principles and particularities. And more. Besides, *Antigone* is the play that Hegel took as his model for understanding tragic conflict, within the Hegelian march of positive change.[80]

Although the play is widely adaptable, the original is not suited for us. If you and I took a time machine to watch *Antigone* in 442 BCE in the theater of Dionysus, we would not be able to respond in harmony with Sophocles' audience. Even if our ancient Greek were fluent, we would be out of place. One example: Sophocles' audience probably believed that Dionysus was brought into presence in the theater by an ode that is sung toward the end of the play to summon him. But you and I don't believe in Dionysus. What can that ode mean for us? It is gorgeous poetry, but can anything like it be effective for a modern audience? You can see what I did with it below (**5.5.2**).

My published translation is an uneasy compromise between page and stage: a text that has two conflicting goals: (a) It aims to meet scholarly standards well enough that teachers who know the original will use it in their classrooms. That means it must satisfy teachers who are looking for a *literary* translation. I have kept exactly to the length of the original, and the line numbers in my version match those in the Greek. (b) It aims to be stageable by today's performers, for today's audience, in the hope that it will not come across as merely a fossil. I have therefore tried to bring across elements of the original that seem most natural in our time, such as line breaks and word emphasis.

My version of the play has partially met both standards. It has been deemed accurate enough for classroom use, and it has often been performed. But, whether it is read in a library or performed on a stage, it cannot give a modern audience what it gave to the ancient Greeks.

5.5.1. Plot

The day before the play opens, the people of Thebes had won a great battle defending themselves from their hereditary enemy, the city of Argos. The Argive army had been led against Thebes by a Theban prince, Polyneices. The sons of Oedipus, Polyneices and his twin brother Eteocles had recently come of age and were supposed to take turns as kings of Thebes. But Eteocles, after his first year as king, refused to cede power to his brother, and so Polyneices had gone for help to Argos. In the battle, the brothers faced off and killed each other. Power then reverted to their uncle Creon, who had been regent when they were too young to rule. Creon has decided to bury Eteocles with full honors, while leaving Polyneices out above ground as punishment for his treason.

In the play's prologue, Antigone opens with torrents of words spilling over from one line to the next, furious at what she takes to be a despotic decree from Creon. Creon has pronounced the death penalty for anyone who buries Polyneices. Antigone's sister Ismene responds in clipped sentences, each line end-stopped, urging Antigone to accept male authority.

Antigone buries her bother symbolically and is arrested. Creon condemns her to death. Soon we will see Creon locked in debate with his son Haemon. Haemon speaks in his father's style until he is prodded into fury during the stichomythia that follows the formal exchange of speeches. He rushes off to try to rescue Antigone, while indicating that he will take his own life. Creon misunderstands and thinks that the threat is against himself.

The blind prophet Tiresias enters to tell Cron he is making a terrible mistake. This makes Creon even more furious. But after Tiresias' exit, the chorus reminds Creon that Tiresias has always been right. Creon has a sudden change of mind and rushes off to set things right. But he is too late. Antigone is already dead, and Haemon takes his own life in front of his father. Creon's wife also will take her life. Creon recognizes that this is all his fault and plunges into grief and regret.

5.5.2. Literary Translation

For the dialogue, in order to ensure that the different voices came through in my version, I translated one character at a time, all through the play. All of Creon, then all of Haemon, and so on. At the end, I rendered all of the choral odes. This approach gave extra life and spin to the stichomythia, where the characters' voices diverge, and the plot changes. Major plot shifts generally occur in Sophocles through stichomythia. Here is an example:

> *Creon:* Is that wrong, showing respect for my job as a leader?
> *Haemon:* You have no respect at all if you trample on the rights of the gods!

> *Creon:* What a sick mind you have: You submit to a woman!
> *Haemon:* No. You'll never catch me giving in to what's shameful.

> *Creon:* But everything you say, at least, is on her side.
> *Haemon:* And on your side! And mine! And the gods below!

And so they have come apart. Haemon will soon take his life, and his father will belatedly see how wrong he was, and then he will grieve.

For the choral odes I have written poems. I was confident that I could do this decently well, because I had been a poet before becoming a scholar, and because I had become satisfied with some of my translations of Horace. I had found that I could rescue what is best in a poem, but not by translating word for word, not by going straight from Latin or Greek words to English ones.

The chorus's entry song rejoices in the victory Thebes won last night over its enemies. Here is one short passage in Sir Richard Jebb's word-for-word translation. It tells of the death of one of the best-known enemies of Thebes:

> Staggered, he fell to the earth with a crash, torch in hand, a man possessed by the frenzy of the mad attack, who just now was raging against us with the blasts of his tempestuous hate (lines 134-37).[81]

I went beyond translating words to give the effect the Greek poem had on me. I made "hurricanes" out of "blasts" and I brought the frenzy of the attacker into an ecstatic dance, as the Greek suggests but does not literally say:

> He crashed to the ground,
> Like a weight slung down in an arc of fire,
> This man who had swooped like a dancer in

ecstasy,
Breathing hurricanes of hatred.

The first stasimon in *Antigone* (the first ode after the entry song) begins with the words *polla ta deina:* many things are *deina.* The word *deinos* can mean both "wonderful" and "terrible." I understand Sophocles to be asking his chorus to sing of the tragic ambiguity of human success. It is both wonderful and terrible. Creon will succeed and deeply regret doing so. My version translates the one word *deina* twice, and this has been imitated by subsequent translators:

Many wonders, many terrors,
But none more wonderful than the human race
Or more dangerous (lines 332-334).

All the odes in this play are stunningly gorgeous. My favorite is the *kletic* ode toward the end, where the chorus sings to summon the god Dionysus into their presence. As the god approaches, the chorus members end their ode with a song of welcome. I think that the spines of the chorus members, and of the audience as well, are shivering as they feel the approach of the god into his sacred space, his theater, and I have not been able to read the Greek without a tingle in my own spine. Here is my poem, which I think has the equivalent effect:

O Leader in the dance of stars
That circle across the night,
Breathing fire,
O shepherd of dark voices,
Child of Zeus, let us see you now.
Come, O Lord, with your throng of Maenads,
Iacchus, steward of joy,
Grant them ecstasy
To dance all night for you. (Lines 1146-1154)

Here is the Jebb translation:

O Leader of the chorus of the stars whose breath is fire, overseer of the chants in the night, son begotten of Zeus, appear, my king, with your attendant Thyiads, who in night-long   frenzy dance and sing you as Iacchus the Giver!

The Greek is spine-tingling. Jebb's prose is accurate, but doesn't have a tingle to it. How could I put the effect of the Greek into English? After several drafts, for example, I finally came to take "overseer of the chants in the night" as "shepherd of dark voices." This is much more powerful than what Jebb had. Still, it speaks to an audience who, like the chorus, believe in the divinity of Dionysus. They also believe that the theater where they sit belongs to his sacred space. This audience expects their god to show up. They have been waiting for this moment since the play began. You and I cannot share their experience, because we don't believe any of that. Is there anything we can do to give an audience of today an experience comparable to the experience of Sophocles' audience? I think so, but it requires a radical translation from one sort of production to another. I can think of several ways to do this. Here is one.

5.6. Translating a Performance of Antigone

The goal is a performance that does for an audience today what we think is most worth rescue. We will leave a lot behind, but that is all right if we rescue a treasure. Here is a suggestion. I start by translating the characters' names, most of which have appropriate meanings in Greek. These need to be translated in order not to leave them as fossils. The original audience knew well what the names meant:

Creon, "ruler, not a legitimate king," translated below as "Bruce Kingman." He is the main figure in the play and shows both despotic tendencies and respect for the opinions of his senate (the chorus).

Antigone, "born to oppose," translated below as "Annie or "Anti."

Ismene, "pleasing," translated below as "Darling."

Haemon, "Bloody," translated below as "Red."

Tiresias, no special Greek meaning, translated below as "the Reverend Rass."

Polyneices, "Quarrelsome," translated below as "Paul" or "Polly."

Eteocles, "True-glory," not used in my proposed translation.

As with *The Misanthrope* we will need an audience and a set of performers who belong to the same community. I suggest high school students or college students. Some of them would have to help in developing the script, since the script should be in language they speak among themselves, and I do not know what they say when I am not present.

Here is the scene I would suggest to them as a starter. They would re-write it. The scene translates the opening of Sophocles' prologue. Here Annie spills out a torrent of words about Kingman's latest decree, and Darling, in clipped lines, insists that women must accept the rule of men. See whether you think this is an equivalent:

Darling: What happened last night? I thought I heard a siren.

Annie: Nothing good, Dar. Uncle Bruce tweeted that anyone who helps Polly will go to jail. Polly will go to jail for ten years, with time off if they give up this idea of becoming a woman. So Polly made another attempt at suicide.

Darling: You mean Paul, don't you? We are not allowed to call him Polly. And he needs to learn to behave as Governor Kingman tells him. You have to stop calling Paul "they."

Annie: No, I mean "Polly." And "they." That's what they want to be called. Polly will never give in. It would violate the very being, the *soul* of Polly. Do I have to call you "Darling?"

Darling: Please call me "Dar." "Darling" makes me think they take my sweetness for granted. And that stuff about Paul's soul is just nonsense. But what happened?

Annie: I checked on Polly before I went to bed, and I saw that they had OD'd again. So I called an ambulance. The medics took them to urgent care and got their stomach pumped. Third time we've saved them. Next time they'll succeed unless we get them away from our uncle. He is always ranting against trans people, and it scares Polly to death. Literally.

I'd have the students start by rewriting this in their idiom, and go on from there. With equivalents (if possible) for the debate between father and son, the execution, the prophetic warning, the suicide, and the recognition scene followed by long grieving. Much will be lost. But I think the most valuable effects can be saved.

Some things must change. Unlike Creon, Kingman would not impose the death penalty for those who help trans people, so we should reduce the penalty to jail time. But the danger of suicide is even more real for us in this situation than it was for Sophocles in his. So the suicides stay.

Polly would be popular in the city. Most people have known Polly since infancy and have accepted Polly's feminine qualities, even if they are anti-trans on principle. Annie too is popular with the citizens because of her relentless honesty and clear thinking. Red is also popular in the city and has his ears open to what the people think. He is engaged to marry Annie, whom he loves. He tries to defend her in a debate with his father, but the debate turns nasty when Kingman uses a gender-based slur against Red. Red storms off threatening suicide. He will try to save Annie first but he finds her dead and soon after he takes his own life.

I want to rescue the scenes in which the ruler takes the blame for his actions and grieves over his losses. To do that I need to bring in religion. I will say that Kingman was converted by an evangelical minister a few years ago and thinks of himself as a Christian. While he is meeting with the leaders of his senate, he has to face the Reverend Rass, who shows up to give urgent advice to his convert: "God wants you to love your neighbor as yourself, and Polly is your neighbor. You are giving them so much pain that they will take their own life unless you start to accept them. Meanwhile, your son Red has gone to say goodbye to Annie in her prison, and after that he will kill himself."

Kingman gets angry and Rass leaves. But then the Senators remind Kingman that Rass had saved the city from terrible mistakes in the past. And Governor Kingman changes his mind, rushes off to save his son Red, but fails. Afterwards he grieves, as Creon grieved.

5.7. Translating with the Help of Artificial Intelligence

Artificial Intelligence is already doing a large share of our translating, from text to text, voice to text, or voice to voice. It is fairly reliable, although not perfect. I recently heard a voice translation of a text of mine featured on the web. There were about a dozen mistakes in only six hundred words. Usually Artificial Intelligence does better. I gave an interview to an Italian newspaper in English, and Artificial Intelligence translated the text from my voice and they published that verbatim. I had this text translated back to an English text by the same means and it was close to what I meant. No major errors. But a translation by Artificial Intelligence should be carefully reviewed on any important matter.

We can expect words-to-words translation by Artificial Intelligence to improve. We can also expect Artificial Intelligence to take on the kind of translation I have offered in the previous section, from a Sophoclean production to one that would have an equivalent effect on an audience of today. I have just proposed translating a conflict about burial, which is a minor issue for us, to a conflict over the treatment of people who reject their birth gender. With the help of Artificial Intelligence we may well find better translations than that, or at least a wider choice.

Artificial Intelligence may be able to provide clear measures for our experiences in theater and out of it. I wrote of the chorus using spine-tingling language in the *kletic* ode. By studying many, many minds, Artificial Intelligence might be able to help us specify what spine-tingling means. Our goal in translating is to create an experience equivalent to that of the original, and experience is felt. We do not feel what happens in the brain. For our purposes, what matters is what we experience in our minds or consciousness. But Artificial Intelligence might be able to draw on its access to vast bodies of knowledge, including brain science, to help us understand our goal by helping us understand our minds. In this context of rescue, at last, we may start to love Artificial Intelligence. It could change its role from threat to helpmate.

What else might Artificial Intelligence do to help us rescue treasures from the past? This is a challenge to the reader, who will know more about Artificial Intelligence than I do now. Everyone will, after all. A few weeks after this book comes out, we will all know more than we did when the book came out, about what Artificial Intelligence can do. So now I hand this over to you, gentle reader. How do you expect to be able to use Artificial Intelligence to meet the necessity of rescue?

So now let's begin.

Appendix: Poems Cited

1. Returning from War, Ten Years After (1970, 1980)
Paul Woodruff
*You should think of what to say <u>before</u> you don't
say it. —Owl*

If you have the feelings, will I find the words?
(Standing together while the children play
in Schenley Park as you put your hand
on mine, behind a tree, on mine
cupped gently at your breast,
and I'm thinking what to say.)

I have lived too long in the silence of birds
before thunder, the hope that time
will turn back and let me stand
on the words I'm chewing, chewing today,
to use when they were best,
to say as I had planned—

ten years ago, past the stillness of birds,
when you had the feelings and I lost the words.

2. Walking on Eggshells
Lucia McKim

After your return
I tried to learn
To walk across them,
Barefoot,
Oh, so carefully,
Step by painful step,
Holding my breath
That I might reach you,
Before the sound of shells
Shattering
Would disappear you back once again
Into that vivid land of War.

3. What the Veteran Said

They taught me weapons, but I never fought;
I was only a clerk, so I told my kids.
But cover my head with a broad-brimmed hat
If I must go out (the veteran said):
The sunshine is clean but I am not.[82]

Those bar girls, to me, were never hot;
I was never there when the whore's hand
Trickled up my thigh till she asked for a drink.
But draw the blinds (the veteran said):
The sunshine is pure and I am not.

I never heard it when the mother caught
A bullet and the small child wailed.
I never saw blood pooling beneath
My friend's stretcher on the Huey's deck.
The sunshine is true and I am not.

The land gives judgment but the sea does not:
That sobbing old woman they detained,
All those sad-eyed prisoners—I never saw a one.
So keep me afloat, I must not touch land,
Where the memories roost that I forgot.

4. Sanctuary

Translate the pagoda. Forget
my odd internal rhyme,
the three-stress line.

But the pagoda, tall as two
palm trees, touched in blue
and gold, half-built, bamboo

crane still swinging, workmen
running for their huts, me
huddling with them. Where the

one-eyed warlord made
his servant call me out
to his safe ditch and said

this was friendly fire. Translate
the shining narrow white
tall-as-two-palms pagoda,

the wrinkled men who built
up, painting as they went,
unsurprised by war.

And the walls I dumbly prayed
would save me when I saw
such misplaced beauty: machine-

gun fire, pagoda rising
white and tall as two palms.
The hope of builders. Translate that.[83]

Bibliography

Works by Paul Woodruff

Most of the research represented in this volume has been published in the works listed by date below.

Articles on Theater

1977. "Rousseau, Moliere, and the Ethics of Laughter," *Philosophy and Literature*, 1. Pp 325-336.

1988. "Engaging Emotion in Theater: A Brechtian Model in Theater History," *Monist,* issue entitled *"Aesthetics and the Histories of the Arts,* ed. by Anita Silvers, Vol. 71. Pp 235-257.

1991. *"Pathei Mathos:* the Thought That Learning is by Ordeal," *Medical Humanities Review* 5. Pp. 7-23.

1997. "The Paradox of Comedy," *Philosophical Topics* 25. Pp 319-35.

2003. "Aesthetics of Theatre," in J. Levinson, ed, *The Oxford Companion to Aesthetics*. Oxford: Oxford University Press. Pp. 594-605.

2011. "Lighting up the Lizard Brain: The New Necessity of Theater." *Topoi* 30.2 (2011). Pp. 151-55. http://www.springerlink.com/openurl.asp?genre=article&id=doi:10.1007/s11245-011-9101-z

2013a. "Theater as Sacrament." *Ramus, Critical Studies in Greek and Roman Literature* 42 (2013): 5-22.

2013b. "Spectator Emotions," in John Deigh, editor, *On Emotions: Philosophical Essays.* New York: Oxford University Press. (Essays published in honor of Robert Solomon) Pp. 59-75.

2014. "Performing Memory: In the Mind and on the Public Stage." In Peter Meineck & David Konstan, eds., *Combat Trauma and the Ancient Greeks.* New York: Palgrave Macmillan. Pp. 286-99.

2017. "Attention to Technique in Theatre." *The Philosophy of Theatre, Drama, and Acting.* Ed. by Tom Stern. London: Rowman and Littlefield International. Pp. 109-121.

2017. "Rhetoric in Tragedy." Chapter 10 in Michael MacDonald, ed., *The Oxford Handbook of Rhetorical Studies*. Oxford: Oxford University Press. Pp. 97-108. 11.

2014. "Performing Memory: In the Mind and on the Public Stage." In Peter Meineck & David Konstan, eds., *Combat Trauma and the Ancient Greeks*. New York: Palgrave Macmillan, 2014. Pp. 286-99.

2018a. "Growing towards Justice." In LeBar, Mark, ed., *Justice*. New York: Oxford University Press. Pp 13-37.

2018b. "Staging Wisdom Through *Hamlet*." In Tzachi Zamir, ed. *Shakespeare's* Hamlet: *Philosophical Perspectives*. Oxford Studies in Philosophy and Literature Series, ed. Richard Eldridge. New York: Oxford University Press. Pp. 46-71.

2024. "Theater as Democracy." Forthcoming in *Philosophy, Analytic Aesthetics, and Theatre*, Michael Bennett, ed. Routledge

Articles on Ancient Theater

2005. "Justice in Translation: Rendering Tragedy" In Gregory, Justina, ed. *A Companion to Greek Tragedy.* Malden, Massachusetts and Oxford: Blackwell Publishing. Pp. 490-504.

2009a. "Aristotle on Character, or, Who is Creon?" *Journal of Aesthetics and Arts Criticism* 67.3. Pp. 301-309.

2009b. "Aristotle's *Poetics:* The Aim of Tragedy." In Georgios Anagnostopoulos, ed., *A Companion to Aristotle.* Malden, Massachusetts and Oxford: Wiley-Blackwell. Pp. 612-27.

2011. "Compassion in Chorus and Audience." *Didaskalia* 8 (2011). Pp 185- 88. *http://www.di-daskalia.net/issues/8/28/*

2012. "The *Philoctetes* of Sophocles," in Kirk Ormand, ed., *A Companion to Sophocles.* Hobeken: Wiley-Blackwell. Pp. 126-140.

2014. "Introduction to the Philoctetes." In *Sophocles: Philoctetes*; Translated by Peter Meineck, with an Introduction by Paul Woodruff. Indianapolis: Hackett, 2014.

2015. "Mimesis." In Pierre Destrée and Penelope Murray, eds., *The Blackwell Companion to Ancient Aesthetics.* Oxford: Wiley-Blackwell. Pp. 329-40.

2016. "Sharing Emotions Through Theater: The Greek Way." *Philosophy East and West* 66.1. Pp 146-51.

2017. "Rhetoric in Tragedy." Chapter 10 in Michael MacDonald, ed., *The Oxford Handbook of Rhetorical Studies.* Oxford: Oxford University Press, 2017. Pp. 97-108.

2018. "Gods, Fate, and Character in the Oedipus Plays." In Woodruff, ed., *The Oedipus Plays of Sophocles: Philosophical Perspectives.* OUP Philosophers on Literature Series, ed. Richard Eldridge. Pp 125-150.

2019a. "Plato's Inverted Theater: Displacing the Wisdom of the Poets." In *Philosophy as Drama: Plato's Thinking through Dialogue.* Editors: Hallvard Fossheim, Vigdis Songe-Møller, and Knut Ågotnes. London and New York: Bloomsbury. Pp. 95-106.

2019b. "Self-Ridicule: Socratic Wisdom." *Laughter and Comedy in Ancient Philosophy,"* ed. by Franco V. Trivigno and Pierre Destrée. New York: Oxford University Press. Pp 165-82.

2020. "Euripides in Translation." *Brill's Companion to Euripides*, ed. by Andreas Markantonatos. Vol II. Leiden: Brill. Pp 1046-64.

2023. "Learning through Love: A Lover's Initiation in the *Symposium*." *The Journal of Ancient Philosophy* (May 2023), 36-58.

Books

2001. *Sophocles' Antigone, Translated with Introduction and Notes.* Indianapolis: Hackett Publishing Company, 2001.

2005. *First Democracy; The Challenge of an Ancient Idea.* New York: Oxford University Press.

2003/2007. Introductions to the plays of Sophocles in the *Theban Plays* and *Four Tragedies.*

2008. *The Necessity of Theater: The Art of Watching and Being Watched.* New York: Oxford University Press.

2011. *The Ajax Dilemma; Justice, Fairness and Rewards.* New York: Oxford University Press.

2014. *Reverence; Renewing a Forgotten Virtue.* New York: Oxford University Press, 2001. Second edition, with a forward by Betty Sue Flowers, as well as two new chapters, and an epilogue: "Sacred Things," "Compassion and Leadership," and "Renewing Reverence." New York: Oxford University Press, 2014. (Translation: Chinese)

2019. *The Garden of Leaders: Revolutionizing Higher Education.* New York: Oxford University Press, 2019.

2022. *Living toward Virtue: Practical Ethics in the Spirit of Socrates.* New York: Oxford University Press, 2022.

Works by Other Authors

1758/1960/1968. *Politics and the Arts: Letter to M. D'Alembert on the Theater,* by Jean-Jacques Rousseau, Translated with Notes and Introduction by Allen Bloom. Agora, 1960; Cornell University Press.

1900/1962. *Sophocles: The Plays and Fragments, Part III, The Antigone,* by Sir Richard Jebb, (3d. edition, 1900). Reprinted 1962. Amsterdam: Servio.

1954. *Molière: The Misanthrope et Tartuffe,* translated into English by Richard Wilbur, (1954). New York: Harcourt Brace.

1977. *The Passions; The Myth and Nature of Human Emotion,* by Robert C. Solomon, (1977). New York: Anchor Books.

2001. *Cicero: The Life and Times of Rome's Greatest Politician,* by Anthony Everitt. New York: Random House, 2001.

2001. *Tyrant: Shakespeare on Politics,* by S. Greenblatt. New York and London: W.W. Norton & Co., 2001.

2001. *Upheavals of Thought; the Intelligence of Emotions,* by Martha C. Nussbaum. Cambridge: Cambridge University Press.

2003, *Sophocles: Theban Plays.* By Peter Meineck and Paul Woodruff, with an introduction by Paul Woodruff. Indianapolis: Hackett Publishing Co.

2007. *Sophocles: Four Tragedies.* By Peter Meineck and Paul Woodruff, with an introduction by Paul Woodruff. Indianapolis: Hackett Publishing Company.

2018. "Darkening the auditorium in the Nineteenth Century British Theatre" by Russell Burdekin. *Theatre Notebook*, 72.1 (2018): 40-57.

2019. *Learning How to Care: An Ethics That Includes the Cognitively Disabled,* by Caroline Christoff. PhD Dissertation at the University of Texas.

2022. *The Tyrant Persuasion: How Rhetoric Shaped the Roman World,* by J. E. Lendon. Princeton: Princeton University Press.

2023. *The Battle for Your Brain: Defending the Tight to Think Freely in the Age of Technology,* by Nita A. Farahany. New York: St. Martin's Press.

Endnotes

Notes are pegged to the text by page number and keyword. Publications are cited by title, date, and author, except in the many cases in which I am citing my own work. If no author is mentioned, I am the author.

[1] Marks, Peter (2023, July 6) Theater is in freefall, and the pandemic isn't the only thing to blame [Editorial]. The Washington Post, https://www.washingtonpost.com/theater-dance/2023/07/06/regional-theater-pandemic-long-wharf/.

[2] https://americanshakespearecenter.com/about/.

[3] *The Knight of the Burning Pestle,* written by Francis Beaumont and performed first in Blackfriars Theater in 1607.

4   For the issues and the need for film to adjust, see: Verma, Prashnu (2023, April 14) AI can make movies, edit actors, fake voices. Hollywood isn't ready [Editorial]. *The Washington Post.* *https://www.washingtonpost.com/technology/2023/04/14/ai-hollywood-filmmaking-dalle/.*

5   A large number of scientists and technology experts signed the following statement on May 30, 2023: "Mitigating the risk of extinction from AI should be a global priority alongside other societal-scale risks such as pandemics and nuclear war."

6   *The Battle for Your Brain: Defending the Right to Think Freely in the Age of Technology,* by Nita A. Farahany (2023).

7   On this see "Theater as Democracy" (2024) and "The *Philoctetes* of Sophocles" (2012).

8   See "Performing Memory: In the Mind and on the Public Stage" (2014) and "Mimesis" (2015).

9   See Chapter Four for a discussion of this, along with "Performing Memory: In the Mind and on the Public Stage" (2014). And check out what James Collins has written on the topic.

10 On plot and character, see my discussion in *The Necessity of Theater* (2008), Chapters 3, 4, and 5.

11 See "Attention to Technique in Theatre" (2017), where I start with this example. We are too awestruck by this long note to think about technique at all.

12 For the insights in this section I am most indebted to Kate Lange.

13 See Chapter 3 on this.

14 See "Darkening the Auditorium" (2018), by Russell Burdekin.

15 For the ideas behind this section I am grateful to Kate Lange.

16 On this topic, see "Theater as Democracy" (2024).

17 Consider also the effect of the nobility's hazing in *Love's Labour's Lost*. There they haze the performers in the formal greeting and the play within a play ("The Nine Worthies"— Scene 5.2). Their heckling ruins every scene aside perhaps from the first (Pompey). Moth is supposed to deliver the formal greeting but the heckling is too much for him: "They do not

mark me, and that puts me out." Because they won't pay attention to him, he keeps messing up his lines (Scene 5.2.2062).

18   In *All is True*," the play that burned down the Globe Theater, Henry VIII is depicted as benign, while Cardinal Wolsey abuses the trust of the king and acts tyrannically. He is put down in a way that is highly satisfying to an audience. As a matter of history, Henry VIII was the most tyrannical of English monarchs, but Shakespeare could not dare to hint at that.

19   See my essay on the Oedipus plays, "Gods, Fate, and Character in the Oedipus Plays" (2018) along with my introductions to all seven of Sophocles' plays, which often depict people with tyrannical features: Meineck and Woodruff, 2003, *Sophocles: Theban Plays* (2003) and *Sophocles: Four Tragedies* (2007).

20   See Greenblatt's *Tyrant: Shakespeare on Politics* (2018).

21   The line is from the Chorus introducing Act 4, line 47 of Henry V. Harry is Henry, who, in disguise, visits the troops at night before the battle. He meets an especially bright and critical soldier named Will, who raises serious questions about the war (Act 4, Scene 1, Lines

92-221). After the battle, Henry treats Will with contempt (Act IV, Scene 7, Line 119 to Scene 8, Line 72). Henry had been lying when he said that, for an ordinary soldier, fighting beside the king ("we few, we happy few") would "gentle his condition" (Act 4, Scene 3, Lines 60-63). He does not treat Will as a gentleman.

22   Laughter: See "Rousseau, Molière and the Ethics of Laughter" (1977). Laughter need not be ridicule. For the idea that ridicule, if used, is best used on oneself, see "Self-Ridicule: Socratic Wisdom" (2019).

23   See *Politics and the Arts: Letter to M. D'Alembert on the Theater,* by Jean-Jacques Rousseau, (1758/1960).

24   Learning: See Chapter 4 and "Rousseau, Molière and the Ethics of Laughter" (1977). From Molière's plays, especially the *Misanthrope,* one can learn much about human foibles and the difficulty of living in society while following principles.

25   Plato, *Gorgias* 449a, ff. https://www.perseus. tufts.edu/hopper/text?doc=Perseus%3Atex-t%3A1999.01.0178%3Atext%3DGorg.%3Asec-tion%3D449a

26   Plato, *Gorgias* 481e, ff.

27   Thucydides *History*, Book 3, Chapter 43.

28   See "Rhetoric in Tragedy," (2017).

29   *Forget the Alamo: The Rise and Fall of an American Myth,* by Burrough, Tomlinson, and Stanford (Penguin, 2021).

30   Nadezhda Mandelstam, *Hope against Hope: A Memoir,* 1970: 22. She made an exception for one friend, the poet Anna Akhmatova.

31   See Lendon's *The Tyrant Persuasion* (2022) and Everitt's *Cicero* (2001).

32   On this, see "Lighting up the Lizard Brain" (2011).

33   On this and other issues with virtual theater, see "Lighting up the Lizard Brain" (2011).

34   On sacred space, see *The Necessity of Theater* (2008), Chapter 6, pp. 108-22; on altar calls, see pp, 121-22.

35   I have argued against the knowledge requirement for virtue in *Living Toward Virtue* (2023a), pp. 9n11, under the valuable influence

of Caroline Christoff, C. E. (2019). *Learning How to Care: An Ethics that Includes the Cognitively Disabled.* University of Texas PhD Dissertation. People who are cognitively disabled should not be barred from the pursuit of virtue.

[36] See "Lighting up the Lizard Brain: The New Necessity of Theater" (2011).

[37] Freedom of agency is a complex subject. In some cases, it is clear that I do or do not have agency. I am at one extreme if I publicly declare my agency. I would be at the other extreme if I were being moved by a force I could not resist: I am a child, and a strong man puts a gun in my hand and pulls the trigger. Children often have no agency. In between are degrees of agency that are hard to assess. I can be deceived or confused about the degree to which I am free as an agent. If a court rules on my guilt or innocence, it will assess my degree of agency. The result may affect my penalty.

Freedom of agency is different from freedom of will. Here I am not writing about freedom of will, a difficult topic. As Kant has argued, and modern science confirmed, we cannot be sure that we have freedom of the will.

[38] See **3.3** below, on Brecht.

39   This section is based on "Spectator Emotions" (2013) For an earlier but similar account of emotions, see *The Necessity of Theater* (2008), pp. 154-57.

40   See *The Passions; The Myth and Nature of Human* Emotion, by Robert C. Solomon, (1977), pp. 185-91—an early statement of views he developed through his later career. An elegant statement of a modern Stoic view of emotion as judgment is given in *Upheavals of Thought; the Intelligence of Emotions,* by Martha C. Nussbaum, (2001), pp. 19 ff., 43-44, and *passim.*

41   See *The Necessity of Theater* (2008), Chapter 9, pp 165-87 on empathy and pp. 167-71 on Brecht.

42   My concepts of virtue and wisdom are Socratic. For details, see E6, *Living toward Virtue,* (2022), esp. pp. 68-74 and 144-46.

43   Only a supernatural being could be truly, flawlessly wise. Human wisdom is inherently flawed, and those who are humanly wise realize this. See E6, *Living toward Virtue,* (2022) especially Chapter 3.

44   This is on the Socratic model of virtue, developed in E6 (2022), esp. pp. pp. 68-74 and 144-45.

45   See A9, "Growing towards Justice," (2018).

46   See C2 and C4.

47   On this see B8, "Plato's Inverted Theater: Displacing the Wisdom of the Poets" (2019) and C3, "Staging Wisdom Through *Hamlet*" (2018).

48   I will treat such questioning below. It is also emphasized in both the Chinese and the Greek traditions. See E6, *Living toward Virtue* (2022), p. 70 and pp. 205-6.

49   I owe this idea to Rick Benitez, who also pointed out that highly intelligent people are often the most likely not to listen, and therefore make awful mistakes. Sophocles and other ancient playwrights knew this well. Think of Oedipus condemning his brother-in-law to death (*Oedipus Tyrannos*), or Creon refusing to listen to his son's report of the opinions of the people he is trying to rule (*Antigone*).

50   Anything just in one way is also unjust in another, and anything fine in one way is also foul in another. See the end of Plato's *Republic* 5.

51   "Staging Wisdom Through *Hamlet*" (2016).

52   On the difference between pity and compassion, see **3.2.1**. The word I translate as compassion has a clearly cognitive element and involves judgment. Pity simply sweeps over us and is independent of judgment.

53   See my article, "The *Philoctetes* of Sophocles" (2012) and my "Introduction to the Philoctetes" (2014).

54   For more on this, see *Living toward Virtue* (2022), Ch. 4.1 on 'moral holidays'.

55   Philosopher Stuart Hampshire interrogated a highly educated German prisoner who had been active in carrying out the holocaust. Hampshire concluded that education is no guarantee of moral behavior. (See E6, *Living toward Virtue* (2022), Chapter 1, p. 9, n. 11).

56   See my opinion piece, "How I healed my soul after returning from Vietnam." *The Washington Post*, January 2-3, 2023. https://www.washingtonpost.com/opinions/2023/01/02/after-vietnam-healing-my-soul/.

57   See *Politics and the Arts: Letter to M. D'Alembert on the Theater*, by Jean-Jacques Rousseau, (1758/1960).

58 See *Living toward Virtue*, (2022), pp. 150-51.

59 See "Rousseau, Moliere, and the Ethics of Laughter," (1977).

60 See "Performing Memory: In the Mind and on the Public Stage" (2014). And check out what James Collins has written on the topic.

61 See *Living toward Virtue* (2022), Chapter 1.

62 See the first poem in the Appendix.

63 "A new artificial intelligence system developed by neuroscience and computer science researchers at The University of Texas at Austin can translate a person's brain activity into a continuous stream of text as the person listens to a story or silently imagines an unfolding narrative. The system relies on extensive training with willing participants and AI similar to ChatGPT, and it could one day help give a voice to people who are mentally conscious yet unable to physically speak. The scientists discuss their innovation on our Point of Discovery podcast and in a college news story about the technology that has captured media attention worldwide." — University of Texas News Release, May, 2023.

64   For performance before a modern audience, the dialogues must be edited especially for length. In Plato's time they would have been presented by a reader or readers, and they may have been performed. We can be sure of this, however: many of the scenes are theatrical. This is especially true of the last speeches of the *Symposium.*

65   On the importance of loving an individual as an individual for this initiation, see *Symposium* 210b6-c6 and "Learning through Love," (2023), pp. 49-51.

66   See "Leaning through Love" (2023).

67   For details on how this works, see *Living toward Virtue* (2022), Appendix 2 to Chapter 6, pp. 181-85.

68   For more on this, see *Living toward Virtue* (2022), Chapter 5.2, p. 116.

69   For Socrates' actions at Delium, see *Living toward Virtue* (2022), Chapter 3.3, p. 65 with n. 9.

70   Thanks to Rick Benitez for this point.

71   See Appendix 4, "Sanctuary," (1985).

72 See F5, *Politics and the Arts: Letter to M. D'Alembert on the Theater,* by Jean-Jacques Rousseau, (1758/1960). On which see D1, 1. "Rousseau, Moliere, and the Ethics of Laughter," *Philosophy and Literature,* 1 (1977), 325-336

73 See F9, *Molière: The Misanthrope et Tartuffe,* translated into English by Richard Wilbur, (1954).

74 I am claiming that *The Misanthrope* is a great play. By that I mean that it has had enormous influence. There may be many plays on similar themes, in languages I do not know, that are better and more effective for their audiences than *The Misanthrope.* In the widest context, *The Misanthrope* may not be a good play. But its influence has been enormous in our culture and in cultures close to ours. It has become a treasure for us, and that is why we want to rescue it through translation. That is why we would be sorry to lose it.

75 See B4, "Justice in Translation: Rendering Tragedy," (2005), and also B12, "Euripides in Translation," (2020).

76 See Winkler, J.J. 1990. "The Ephebes' Song: Tragôidia and Polis." In Winkler and Zeitlin, eds. *Nothing to Do with Dionysos? Athenian Drama in Its Social Context.* Princeton: 20–62.

77   After a battle in their civil war, an Athenian on the democratic side could say this to oligarchs during a brief truce: "Why are you driving us out of the city? ... We used to dance together!" Xenophon, *Hellenika*, 2.4.20-21.

78   As with *The Misanthrope*, I am calling the *Antigone* a treasure. We would hate to lose it. It is a great play in the sense that it has had great influence, and through that influence it has become important in many cultures. I make no claims here about its quality relative to plays on similar themes in languages I do not know.

79   Two famous examples: Anouilh's *Antigone* (Paris, 1944) and Nelson Mandela's performance as Creon (late 1960's).

80   Hegel is easily misunderstood on this subject. See E7, *Sophocles' Antigone* (2001), pp, 63-65.

81   Sophocles Part III, *Antigone*, by Sir Richard Jebb (1900/1962).

82   In Euripides' *Heracles Furens*, Heracles covers his head so as not to pollute the sun by contact with him, after what he has done. In afterwar madness, he has killed his children.

83   The pagoda still stands, near Tinh Bien, in the Delta near Vietnam's border with Cambodia. The paint was chipped when I visited it in 2002. It was built as a prayer for peace. About a mile away is the rock team house where my friends were blown up while waiting for the help from me that I was unable to deliver.